SERIES EDITOR: LEE JOHNSON

OSPREY MILITARY WARRIOR

ITALIAN MILITIAMAN
1260–1392

TEXT BY
DAVID NICOLLE PhD

COLOUR PLATES BY
CHRISTA HOOK

OSPREY
MILITARY

First published in Great Britain in 1999 by Osprey Publishing,
Elms Court, Chapel Way, Botley, Oxford OX2 9LP, United Kingdom

ISBN 1 85532 826 7

Military Editor: Nikolai Bogdanovic
Design: Alan Hamp

Origination by Renaissance, Bournemouth, UK
Printed through World Print Ltd., Hong Kong

99 00 01 02 03   10 9 8 7 6 5 4 3 2 1

FOR A CATALOGUE OF ALL TITLES PUBLISHED BY OSPREY MILITARY,
AUTOMOTIVE AND AVIATION PLEASE WRITE TO:

The Marketing Manager, Osprey Publishing, PO Box 140,
Wellingborough, Northants NN8 4ZA, UK

OR VISIT OSPREY'S WEBSITE AT
http://www.osprey-publishing.co.uk

Dedication

For the late John Beeler – a gentleman, a scholar and a soldier.

Editor's Note

Numerous foreign and technical terms appear in italics throughout
the text. For ease of reference, an explanation of these key
recurrent terms can be found in the *Glossary* section, towards
the end of the book.

Publishers' Note

Readers may wish to study this title in conjunction with the following
select list of Osprey publications:

MAA 50 *Medieval European Armies*
MAA 75 *Armies of the Crusades*
MAA 94 *The Swiss at War 1300–1500*
MAA 99 *Medieval Heraldry*
MAA 136 *Italian Medieval Armies 1300–1500*
MAA 151 *The Scottish and Welsh Wars 1250–1400*
MAA 166 *Medieval German Armies 1300–1500*
MAA 171 *Saladin and the Saracens*
MAA 200 *El Cid and Reconquista 1050–1492*
MAA 210 *Venetian Empire 1200–1670*
MAA 231 *French Medieval Armies 1000–1300*
MAA 251 *Medieval Chinese Armies 1260–1520*
MAA 287 *Byzantine Armies 1118–1461*
Elite 19 *The Crusades*
Elite 28 *Medieval Siege Warfare*
Warrior 11 *English Longbowman 1250–1513*
Warrior 18 *Knight of Outremer 1187–1344*
Campaign 43 *Fornovo 1495*
Campaign 44 *Pavia 1525*

Artist's Note

Readers may care to note that the original paintings from which the
colour plates in this book were prepared are available for private
sale. All reproduction copyright whatsoever is retained by the
Publishers. All enquiries should be addressed to:

Scorpio Gallery
PO Box 475, Hailsham, East Sussex BN27 2SL

The Publishers regret that they can enter into no correspondence
upon this matter.

TITLE PAGE **A foot soldier with a very early form of visored
bacinetto, as shown on a late-13th-century carved relief.
(Pinacoteca Comunale, Sansepolcro)**

ITALIAN MILITIAMAN
1260–1392

ITALY – A EUROPEAN ANOMALY

Italy was very different to the rest of Europe in the medieval era. There were also extreme regional differences within its physical confines. Though feudalism had developed along the same lines as elsewhere, Italy was highly urbanised and many of its regions were exceptionally well populated. The Black Death of the mid-14th century had devastated some areas, but the populations of both the centre and north were quick to revive. Southern Italy, meanwhile, continued to witness the abandonment of villages. Rural poverty was a major feature of life: huge numbers of wandering beggar families roamed the countryside, and banditry was commonplace.

Italy's mountain valleys flourished during the Middle Ages and the farmers and semi-nomadic pastoralists inhabiting them were regarded as good military recruits. Armies from the urbanised lowlands drew many soldiers, particularly crossbowmen, from these primitive mountain communities. By contrast to the small, impoverished settlements of rural areas, Italy's great cities were not only wealthy but also powerful and densely populated. Late-13th-century Verona, for example, had a population of some 40,000 people; Florence's stood at around 95,000; and Lucca, Siena and Pisa each had around 28,000 inhabitants. Italy as a whole had a population of around twelve million, compared to the four million of England.

The disparate nature of life in medieval Italy was also evident on the country's peripheral islands. Sardinia and Corsica had remained primitive. On the former, the rival maritime republics, principally Pisa and Genoa, battled for control, while the indigenous Sards played a significant military role in the service of their foreign rulers. Meanwhile in Sicily the Muslim population had been converted, expelled or forcibly relocated to a mainland outpost around the massive royal castle of Lucera, where Arab–Islamic culture continued to flourish. The Orthodox Greek population was also in decline, as was the Jewish one. Sicily had degenerated from a rich centre of Mediterranean trade to an impoverished backwater wracked by violence. During the 14th century, forests reclaimed the centre of the island and hunting became a major economic activity.

'The Poor driven from Siena in 1328–30' as shown in a mid-14th-century Florentine manuscript. Note the shields with the arms of Siena over the gate. (Ms. Tempi 3.c, f. 57v, Bib. Laurenziana, Florence; photo. Alberto Scardigli)

By the 12th century, most of the cities which feature so strongly in medieval Italian history had adopted the model of the *comune*. Typically this process began when a city's leading citizens formed a *coniuratio* (an association sworn to maintaining peace and working for the common good). The *coniuratio* then merged with the *arengo* (the town assembly) to form a *comune*. A further development of this process occurred when cities set about dominating their surrounding villages, thus establishing a much wider sphere of sovereignty called a *contado*.

Throughout the 11th–12th centuries many Italian cities were dominated by rich patrician families, while military matters came under the control of the *capitani* and the knightly *valvassori*. The first social group to further the interests of its members was that of the *miles* or knights, followed by that of the leading merchants. These groups were represented by *consuli*, who were normally answerable to a larger general council and ultimately to a parliament of all citizens.

Leading aristocrats were often locked in bitter feuds, and this led to the building of tall *torri* (privately fortified towers) in the cities, some of which can still be seen today. Violence, in particular the resolution of the *vendetta*, became such a problem in the 13th century that many cities were desperate to free themselves from rule by the troublesome consular aristocracies. During the 13th and 14th centuries some cities took the drastic step of switching from the *comune* to corporate government. However, the frequent failure of such 'constitutional' systems led to authority residing with a single man and his descendants, a system known as the *signoria*. This was initially established in time of crisis when the authority of a single man (a *signore*) seemed the only way of dealing with chronic social and political problems, military defeats and lawlessness, but in many areas the tyrant's rule firmly established itself. Some *signori* came from local aristocratic families: other *signori* families were non-nobles that had been amassing wealth for generations. All maintained their authority through military power.

A – Aragonese
E – Este
E/P – Este under Papal suzerainty
G – Genoese
P – Papal
S – Della Scala
V – Visconti
VN – Venetian

ITALY c.1336

BELOW LEFT **Ermanno da Sassoferrato, the *Capitano del Popolo* of Perugia in 1278.**

BELOW RIGHT **Matteo da Corriggia di Parma, the *Podestà* in 1278. Both of these are the work of Nicola or Giovanni Pisano. (*In situ*, Fontana Maggiore, Perugia)**

Fortunately there were several other systems of government in medieval Italy. The *Podestà* system came about when rivalry between powerful families disrupted daily and commercial life to such an extent that a paid official was brought in to maintain law and order for a fixed period. The *popolo* form of government usurped the power of the former dominant families, but it did not represent the majority as one might expect: instead it championed the cause of the 'new rich' merchant class. Once in power, they drew up laws which reduced the influence of the 'old rich'. The *popolo* system reached its peak in the mid-13th century, drawing representatives from leading merchant guilds, though not from the ranks of humble craftsmen. In Florence in 1250, a typical *popolo* took control of the city. The *societas populi*, or 'society of the [non-aristocratic] people', formed the Primo Popolo ('first popular' government) based upon the interests of commercial groups and the infantry militia. Florence, like many other cities, also appointed a *Capitano del Popolo*, or leader of the militia forces, as a counterweight to the more established *Podestà*. However, this did not end factional fighting, and eventually the guild-based *Priori* oligarchy took over, governing Florence with considerable success throughout the 14th century. Meanwhile in the rival city of Siena a similar oligarchy of merchant bankers called the *Noveschi* held power from 1287 until 1355. Many other cities went through a similar process.

Political tensions came in several forms. There were tensions not only within cities but also between a city and its *contado*, which was a vital source of both food and military manpower. Cities tried to nibble away at their rivals' *contado*, sometimes through economic warfare, sometimes through the use of military force. Later in the 14th century the process was taken a step further: mountain regions were occupied by the cities in order to control trade routes and exploit iron mines for their arms industries. Weaker cities struggled to avoid being taken over by bigger ones. For example, Lucca tried so hard not to antagonise its powerful neighbour that it was forced to accept humiliating treaties.

Medieval Italy was also divided between Ghibellines and Guelfs. The former saw the German Emperor as Italy's best defence in a hostile world: the latter perceived the Emperor as a threat and thus supported the Papacy's bid for temporal power. By the 1330s, however, such a general distinction meant little, and any factional differences merely reflected local rivalries. In fact the Papacy was virtually taken over by France in the 14th century, the Popes submitting to their exile in Avignon from 1309 until the 15th century. The Papal territories as yet hardly existed as a state. Instead they comprised a collection of autonomous enclaves recognising some degree of Papal sovereignty. It was the Kingdom of Naples further south that was the largest (but not necessarily the most powerful) state in Italy. Here the feudal system proved strong enough to maintain control over scattered cities, many of which fell into decline while those of the north flourished.

Another remarkable characteristic of medieval Italy was its far-flung overseas trade, which had a significant impact on its scientific and cultural awareness. The link between Genoa and the Islamic world had been strong since at least the 12th century. Both Venice and Genoa established colonies in the eastern Mediterranean, Aegean and Black Seas. Meanwhile southern Italy still had close links with the Balkans. Italian merchants ranged across medieval Russia and visited China until the fall of the Mongol Yüan dynasty disrupted such contacts. Even so Genoese relations with the Mongol Khans of southern Russia remained strong, despite occasional clashes of interest in the Crimea.

These wide-ranging contacts also appear to have had a significant impact on arms, armour and advanced tactical theory. The crossbow and eyeglass were particularly useful new developments, and there were advances too in maritime technology. By the 11th century Lombardy had a close knowledge of both Byzantine and Islamic military technology, notably in the use of crossbows in siege warfare. In the late-12th century, classical Greek and Roman military texts were translated by Gherardo of Cremona. This scholarly interest in military matters continued through the 13th and 14th centuries, resulting in the writing of new treatises which reflected Byzantine Greek and Arab–Islamic influences. In fact the

BELOW **The medieval waterfront of the city of Cefalu in Sicily, a rare surviving example that demonstrates how houses built on earlier fortifications came right down to the sea's edge. (Author's photograph)**

whole area covering northern Italy, southern France and the Iberian peninsula witnessed a flourishing of military experimentation.

CHRONOLOGY

(Note: **Gh** = Ghibelline 'Imperial party'; **Gu** = Guelf 'Papal party')

1250	Death of Emperor Frederick II (Gh), collapse of Imperial power in Italy; appointment of the first *Capitano del Popolo* in Florence (Gu) marks official entry of militia into politics.
1259	Este family (Gu) takes control of Ferrara as *signori*.
1260	Siena (Gh) defeats Florence (Gu) at Montaperti.
1263	Mastino della Scala becomes *Podestà* of Verona; Della Scala family (Gh) retains control of Verona as *signori* until 1387.
1265–66	Charles of Anjou (Gu), invited to Italy by Pope Clement IV to evict German Imperial forces from Italy, defeats King Manfred (Gh) at Benevento.
1268	Charles of Anjou (Gu) defeats and executes King Manfred (Gh) at Tagliacozza, and becomes King of Naples and Sicily.
1275	Guido Novello (Gh) defeats Guelf force near Faenza.
1278	Consolidation of Papal authority in the Marches.
1282	Membership of the Chief Magistracy of Florence is confined to members of the *Arti* (trade guilds).
1282	Sicilian Vespers uprising in Sicily against Angevin–French of Naples; Peter III of Aragon is invited to rule.
1283	Crusade proclaimed against Aragonese domination of Sicily.
1287	Government of Siena reorganised under the *Noveschi* (the Nine)
1288	Este family (Gu) take control of Modena as *signori*.
1289	Florence defeats Arezzo at Battle of Campaldino.
1293	Appointment of the first *Gonfaloniere di Giustizia* to maintain order in Florence; guilds take responsibility for equipment of militia in Padua.

1294	Boniface VIII becomes Pope (1294–1303) and attempts to impose Papal hegemony upon Italy; reorganisation of Venetian militias.
1295	Ottone Visconti becomes Archbishop and effective ruler of Milan; Visconti family eventually become *signori* of Milan.
1296	Open quarrel between France and Papacy.
1300	King Charles of Naples orders forcible conversion of Muslim community in Lucera.
1302	War between Angevins and Aragonese concludes with recognition of Angevin rule on the mainland, and Aragonese rule in Sicily.
1303	Emperor accepts principle that the Pope is superior to the Emperor; French and Italian supporters kidnap Pope at Anagni.
1304	Regulations governing *contado* infantry incorporated into the constitution of Siena; reorganisation of the militia in Padua.
1305	Catalan mercenaries arrive in Italy.
1308	Henry VII (Gh) becomes Emperor (1308–13) but fails in attempts to unite Italy by force.
1309	Start of the 'Babylonish Captivity' when Pope Clement V transfers Papacy from Rome to Avignon.
1309–10	Crusade preached against Venice.
1310	Council of Ten oligarchy appointed in Venice.
1311	Visconti (Gh) *signoria* confirms its domination of Milan and steadily increases the size of the Milanese state; alliance of Guelf cities formed to resist Emperor Henry VII.

1313	Robert of Anjou (Gu), King of Naples (1309–43), begins unsuccessful attempt to unite Italy by force.
1316–28	Lucca, under Castruccio Castracani, dominates western Tuscany.
1318	Rioting by Sienese militia.
1321	Crusade launched against Ferrara (Gh), Milan (Gh) and Ghibelline sympathisers in Spoleto and the Marches; extended to include Mantua (Gh) in 1324.
1325	Bologna defeated by Modena at Zappollino; Florentine militia defeated by Lucca at Altopascio.
1325–26	War between Angevins of Naples and Aragonese of Sicily.
1326–28	Unsuccessful invasions of Italy by German Emperor Ludwig IV.
1337	New laws drawn up in Florence concerning hire of mercenaries.
1339	Venice annexes Treviso and begins its domination of the neighbouring mainland.

1340	Election of first Doge (Duke) of Genoa.
1342	Walter de Brienne, titular Duke of Athens, appointed ruler of Florence (later forced out in 1343); Florence remains a republic.
1347	Cola di Rienzi attempts to revive the Roman Republic as a focus for Italian unity.
1347–48	Black Death reaches Italy.
1350	Giovanni Visconti of Milan attacks Florence; Papal forces campaigning in the Romagna; Savoy defeats Swiss at Siôn.
1353–57	Crusades to regain control of Papal States in central Italy.
1354	Crossbowmen reorganised as a separate part of the Florentine militia; Spoleto incorporated into Papal States; militia of Milan defeat mercenary company of Conrad of Landau in service of Mantua.
1357	Savoy takes Verrua from Marquis of Monferrato.
1358	Mercenary Grand Company defeated while crossing Florentine territory.
1360	Crusade against Milan (renewed in 1363 and 1368); Peace of Brétigny between France and England (100 Years War) results in large numbers of unemployed mercenary troops arriving in Italy.
1363	Mercenary English White Company defeat Florentine militia.
1364	Florentine militia defeats White Company.
1366	League of central Italian cities against freebooting mercenary companies.
1367	Genoa seizes Corsica.
1367–70	Papacy temporarily returns to Rome from 'Babylonish Exile' in Avignon.
1372–73	War between Venice and Padua, and between Venice and Hungary.
1377	Papacy returns to Rome.
1378	Ciompi uprising by the *Popolo Minuto* (minor guilds) and artisans in Florence temporarily breaks the power of the Guelfs and the *Popolo Grasso* (greater guilds).
1378–81	Venice defeats Genoa.
1378–1417	Great Schism with two rival Popes.
1382	*Popolo Grasso* regains political power in Florence and forms an oligarchy.
1385–1402	Gian Galeazzo Visconti almost succeeds in uniting northern and central Italy by force.
1387	Padua defeats Verona at Castagnaro.
1390–1404	Resistance movement under Élénore of Arborea against Aragonese in Sardinia.
1392	End of war between Florence and Milan.

Troops disembarking from a ship in the face of resistance from lightly armoured archers, taken from the early-14th-century Franco–Italian *Libre des Roumans; Histoire Iulius Cesar.* (Cod. Marc. Fr. Z.3, f.49v, Biblioteca Marciana, Venice; photograph by Foto Toso)

THE CROSSBOW

The crossbow was not a new invention of the Middle Ages. It had been used both in ancient China (where it remained a vital infantry weapon) and in pre-Roman Greece. However, it survived in Europe only as a complex frame-mounted siege machine or as a small hunting weapon. Chinese influences via Central Asia may have stimulated a revival in the use of handheld crossbows in 10th-century Arab–Persian armies. However, it is unclear whether there was any connection between this Islamic re-introduction and the use of handheld crossbows in 11th-century Spain, southern France and Alpine Italy, while mention of crossbows in 10th-century Scandinavia could reflect the Vikings' close commercial links with Islamic Iran. The significance of a surviving late-Roman hunting crossbow is also a matter of debate. It has little in common with earlier Greek weapons but appears similar to medieval Middle Eastern crossbows. Other references to crossbows in 10th-century northern France may be descriptions of frame-mounted siege weapons.

The late-12th century saw important technical improvements, notably the ability to make accurate revolving nuts from horn or bone using a pole-lathe. This technological advance, along with a considerable increase in siege warfare in the 11th–12th centuries, led to the crossbow becoming a truly revolutionary and decisive weapon on land as well as at sea.

Added impetus came from the widespread replacement of one-piece wooden bows with more powerful composite constructions. This was not an entirely new approach to bow-making. Oriental crossbow-makers had used composite construction in handbows for some time. Until recently it was thought that, although the Europeans copied the basic idea of composite construction, the finer details of this method of bow-making were neglected. Further evidence of this could be found in subtle differences in the way Oriental handbows and European crossbows were put together. However, a recent discovery of medieval Islamic composite crossbows in Syria has shown that Muslim craftsmen themselves used different techniques to make crossbows and handbows.

The first specific references to crossbows in Italy are to be found in Pisa in 1162 and Genoa in 1181: both of these cities were naval powers trading with the east. By the mid-13th century crossbows had been widely adopted as a naval and infantry weapon across northern Italy. A new style of warfare employing large numbers of crossbow-armed infantry suited the small but wealthy Italian cities. Disciplined, spear-armed infantry militias from northern Italy had already broken the German Empire's bid to dominate the country. The crossbow, which required little strength and

'Martyrdom of St. Sebastian', a mid-14th-century panel painting by Giovanni del Biondo. (Museo dell'Opera del Duomo, Florence; photograph Niccolò Orsi Battaglini)

modest training, now enabled part-time militiamen to become an even more effective fighting force. As a result, in medieval Europe the Italian crossbowman became as feared as the English longbowman.

One major criticism levelled against the crossbow was that its rate of shooting was too slow, but this has been exaggerated. Of course, it could not shoot as fast as a handbow, yet the early crossbow was not as slow as some suggest. In fact it was only in the late-14th and 15th centuries, with the adoption of complicated mechanical spanning devices, that the crossbow's rate of fire slumped. In return, however, these new spanning devices provided a power which longbows and even early handguns could not beat. Nevertheless the crossbow's limitation led to the establishment of a new corps of *pavesari* carrying large mantlet shields, whose job it was to protect the crossbowman as he reloaded.

Handbows and crossbows were also used differently. Handbows could be aimed at individual targets, but were more usually employed as massed-fire weapons, showering large numbers of arrows into a predetermined killing zone. Though the crossbow offered an ever increasing power-to-weight ratio, the fact that it was held horizontally meant that it could not provide a 'falling barrage' of arrows. Tactically it was like the single-shot musket, multiple volleys only being possible if separate ranks shot in sequence. The arrows and bolts shot from a crossbow were also far more efficient than those despatched from a handbow. The latter used long arrows, which were subject to lateral stress around the bow when released and consequently quivered during the first phase of flight. The crossbow bolt was projected in a straight line, and because it lay on top of the crossbow's stock it did not need to be as long as an arrow. These stubbier more aerodynamic bolts also gave improved accuracy, range and armour-piercing capability.

The increasing use made of crossbows had a clear impact upon armour. This was especially the case in Italy, where face-covering

Naval battle between Caesar and the Britons in the *Codice Sallustiana* made in Bologna in 1320–30. Note the crossbowmen in both ships and the special rigging-cutting weapons. (Ms. Rici. 1538, c.12, Biblioteca Riccardiana, Florence)

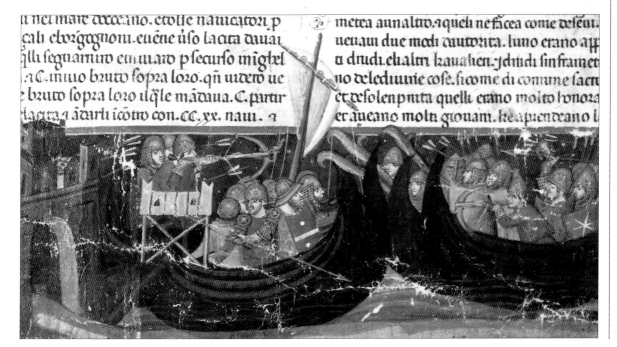

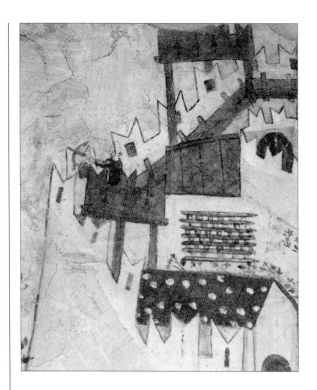

Detail of a crude wall-painting of a castle, made around 1340, showing additional wooden towers within the main wall. (*In situ*, Avio castle; author's photograph)

The top of the main tower of Avio castle with defences at two levels covered. (Author's photograph)

helmets, heavier body protection and horse armour were re-introduced. The demand for armour gave a boost to the iron industry and led to experimentation with lighter materials, including leather. *Cuir-bouilli* (hardened leather armour) was more widely used in late-13th and 14th-century Italy than in other parts of western Europe. It is also interesting to note that crossbows were used to test armour from at least 1341, when a '*corratiae de mediâ probâ*' (a half-proofed cuirass) was mentioned.

Paradoxically, the boost that the crossbow gave to Italian armour technology was so successful that the crossbow itself fell out of favour in the 14th century, and heavy cavalry became the dominant force in the battlefield once more. Its popularity was gradually re-established, although the newer versions were more complex, more expensive to manufacture, and had a reduced rate-of-fire. In Italy the adoption of crossbows by infantry units had already led to changes in military ideas and organisation: this in turn made the adoption of firearms in the late-14th and 15th centuries a much easier affair. There had been a genuine 'crossbow revolution' and it had taken warfare out of the hands of the aristocracy.

Crossbow versions and spanning systems

A distinct disadvantage of early medieval crossbows was that they were cumbersome. The main advantages such weapons had over hand-held bows though was that they could be left under tension for long periods, and were relatively easy to shoot accurately. The early style of bow survived as large 'wall crossbows', often using a simple peg to release the string rather than a revolving nut and being made mostly of yew or ash. Other woods mentioned in the manufacture of crossbows are laburnum, willow, hazel, elm, maple and cyprus, though most of these were used in the stock rather than the bow.

Crossbows of composite construction (employing materials such as horn and sinew) may have reached Europe as early as the end of the 12th century, but were certainly in use in Genoa by the mid-13th century. Composite construction gave a much greater power-to-weight ratio, because sinew has a tensile strength approximately four times that of wood, and horn has a similarly better compression ratio: however, wood was still used to make the core of the bow. The bow on a crossbow was considerably shorter, thicker and endured more prolonged stress than that of a handheld bow. This may explain why in Europe the strips of horn were usually set edgeways along the bow rather than flat, and why the wooden core continued to take a greater proportion of stress. Up to half the entire mass could consist of animal sinew, a far greater proportion than in oriental composite handbows. Many European composite crossbows also incorporated strips of whalebone fastened with fish glue. Another system consisted of a core made from strips of horn and whalebone, separated by horn and with lengths of spruce on each side. Crossbow strings were usually made of linen or hemp, and were sometimes waxed to reduce wear and tear. As construction methods improved and the bows became stronger, so the length of their pull fell from between 80–90cm to 15–20cm. As a result, the stock of the bow was strengthened with bone, horn or iron, in order not to compromise the power stored in the span.

A further development saw the use of steel to make the bow. As early as 1086, a weapon with a blue 'metallic' bow appears in a Mozarab Spanish manuscript: given the Islamic world's superiority at this time in this type of metallurgy, the evidence appears convincing enough to indicate that it might be of steel. There is also evidence of experimentation with steel crossbows in southern France in the late-13th century. The first clear reference to a steel bow dates from 1314, and it is described as being 'in the Genoese manner'. These early steel crossbows were no doubt prone to failing spectacularly, and it is not until the 1370s that we find such weapons in regular military use.

The earliest method of spanning or pulling back a crossbow was to place one foot on each arm of the bow and then draw back the string. In the late-12th century the belt hook appeared in Egypt, and then in Mediterranean Europe shortly after. The resultant *balestra a crocco* allowed the bowman to use the full strength of his legs, and enabled him to achieve a maximum pull of around 150 kilograms. The next development saw the incorporation of a pulley onto the belt hook strap. The

BELOW LEFT **Detail from the wall-painting by Altichiero portraying the life of St. James, c. 1370, showing the Battle of Clavigo: a crossbowman and an archer with a simple bow are both distinguishable. (*In situ*, Chapel of San Giacomo, the Basilica, Padua; author's photograph)**

BELOW RIGHT **Another detail from Altichiero's life of St. James: the companions of the saint are taken before the King of Spain. (Author's photograph)**

The outer circuit walls of Angera castle overlooking Lake Maggiore. This style of Italian fortification was also to be found in the Balkans and Crusader Greece. (Author's photograph)

earliest Italian reference to a 'one foot crossbow' (almost certainly with a stirrup lashed to the end of the stock) comes from Piacenza in 1269, though the device had probably been around for some time. An astonishing amount of detail on this subject lay preserved in the royal archives of Naples, but unfortunately this was lost in American bombing during the Second World War. Some documents had already been published beforehand, including the lists of weaponry ordered by King Charles for his war against the Aragonese. In 1282, for example, the king required *balestre de fusto* (wooden crossbows) of both the 'one foot' and 'two feet' varieties (though only half as many of the latter), plus *balestre de corno* (composite crossbows), again of 'one foot' and 'two feet' types. A huge number of bolts were needed for the 'one foot' crossbows and a third as many for the 'two feet'. We also know that 20 wooden 'one foot' crossbows were sent to one castle, along with 'bandoliers' (probably shoulder-belt spanning devices for use on horseback: there are many references to mounted crossbowmen in 13th-century Italy). A *balestra de torno* (a windlass crossbow) and 400 bolts were also sent to the same castle.

The 14th century saw the appearance of several ingenious spanning devices, such as the *gaffle*. Its associated crossbow, generally known as a *balestra a leva*, could be used on horseback, and was in widespread use from the mid-14th century. The more complicated *cranequin* (also known as a 'rack' or 'cric') first appeared around 1373, but it was too expensive and delicate to be used effectively in war. The spanning windlass was like a miniaturised version of the system used to span frame-mounted siege crossbows since Roman times: the *balestra de torno* was widely used in sieges and was probably spanned like this. Finally, there was the 'great crossbow', surviving examples of which measure 1.5–2 metres in length. Comparable weapons had been used in the Byzantine and Islamic worlds for centuries, and these were all probably spanned by winches and mounted on wooden pedestals or frames. The '*scagni pro balistis a torno*' mentioned in a source from Italian-influenced Dubrovnik in 1376 may well have been such a pedestal.

The Italian crossbow-like siege weapon called the *spingarda* was the same as the French *espringal*, the English *springald* and the Arabic *qaws al-ziyar*. These weapons had two separate bow-arms and derived their power from twisted skeins of horse-hair, sinew or other such material. The *spingarda* normally shot *viretoni*, which were 'spinning' bolts similar to those used in the largest *balestre de torno*. Apart from commonly used crossbow types, there are also records of experimental versions. Multiple or multi-shot crossbows were used in medieval China, and references to them can be found in 12th-century Egypt. A similar device capable of shooting 15 arrows is mentioned in a 12th-century Venetian source, and (more realistically) an eight-bolt multiple-shot Venetian crossbow is described in a document dating from 1411. However, only China brought such devices into practical use. (See Plate E for illustrated details of crossbow spanning methods and mechanisms.)

FROM MILITIAMAN TO PROFESSIONAL

Urban militias were the main forces at the disposition of the Italian cities, whereas *masnada* levies or militias were the main source of military muscle availiable to the feudal lords of the surrounding area. Most feudal infantry (*pedites*) were of servile origin and a large proportion were non-combatants, including *guastatori*, whose primary role was to destroy enemy crops. Those who fought in battle tended to be conscripted freemen or mercenaries, many of whom were archers. For freemen, such service was a privilege and duty, yet the laws they served under were very different to those upheld by the knightly cavalry. In the 12th and early-13th centuries fighting with bows and crossbows was still regarded as 'lower-class warfare' by both the knights and by the spear-armed urban infantry militiamen who fought in close combat. It took many years for crossbowmen to achieve élite status: unfortunately, by this time the crossbow was no longer a decisive tactical weapon.

'Soldiers at the Crucifixion' on a damaged wall-painting from c. 1330–35. (*In situ*, church of Sant' Abbondio, Como; author's photograph)

Urban militias were conscripted when circumstances dictated, and were composed of noble cavalry, non-noble cavalry (from the wealthier middle class) and infantry (mostly from the middle class and artisans). Cities could also call upon men from their surrounding area – the local rural aristocracy often had a quasi-feudal relationship with the city, regarding it as their surrogate 'lord'. The laws governing conscription, training, mustering and arming were very precise and were written into the city's constitution. They were also modified in response to military and political changes. Mercenaries had long been present in urban armies, and they continued to play a role. The really poor, however, were rarely involved in such matters.

Urban knights had been integrated into the militia since the 10th century. Nevertheless the infantry now dominated, not only numerically (a proportion of ten *pedites* to one knight was the norm) but also politically: the *milites* were no longer dominant and they could not afford to despise the *pedites*, who wielded political power. Such circumstances meant that Italian communal armies were at the forefront of a revival in effective tactical co-ordination between cavalry and infantry during the 11th and 12th centuries. But the static, spear-armed infantry militias were themselves threatened by the crossbow since they provided an even easier target than the cavalry. To survive, communal militias had to change. The result was the adoption of the crossbow as a key weapon, and the creation of the new force of *pavesari*, who shielded the crossbowmen as they reloaded, and provided a base from which light infantry and cavalry could launch their charges. Almost identical tactics had already been adopted in the Middle East to deal with the threat posed by mounted archers armed with composite bows.

Italian cities were in a good position to be able to take full advantage of the crossbow's potential. Most were wealthy, their arms-manufacturing facilities were well established, and levels of political sophistication were high. The crucial factor above all though was that military discipline was built upon existing bonds of communal loyalty. The division of cities into quarters or wards for militia recruitment facilitated the establishment of a military framework: the number of such quarters varied from city to city but they remained a fundamental feature of medieval Italian urban life.

Italian militias reached a peak in the 13th century, after which their discipline was eroded by diverging interests of the rich and the less prosperous, and between employer and employee. Militia service became less prevalent in some northern cities in the first half of the 13th century, but in Tuscany it remained the norm until well into the 14th century. Meanwhile other factors were also at work. During the first half of the 13th century freebooting and 'Crusader' armies campaigned across much of Italy. Several included large numbers of so-called 'Saracens' from Lucera. This extraordinary ghetto of Italian Muslims, forcibly transferred from Sicily in the 13th century, survived by serving as soldiers for whichever ruler offered them protection. They included cavalry but were most often employed as light infantry armed with composite bows and crossbows. Their offensive infantry tactics had a remarkable influence upon Italian infantry militias and, through them, on the whole development of medieval European infantry warfare in the 13th and 14th centuries. One thing urban militias could not reproduce was the Lucera 'Saracens' skill with the composite handbow. Nevertheless, militias were expected to be proficient in the use of weapons, be they armoured cavalry, light cavalry, *pavesari* mantlet-bearers, *scuderi* 'small shield' infantry, *balestieri* crossbowmen, or the increasingly common mounted crossbowmen.

The Piazza del Duomo in the Tuscan hilltop town of San Gimignano, showing the Torri dei Salvucci. (Author's photograph)

The 14th century was a period of decline for communal militias, and by the 1390s they had virtually disappeared in many cities. Yet this decline varied from place to place, and crossbowmen were less affected than cavalry or other foot soldiers: it was also a decline that mirrored that of Italian urban political liberties in this period. Tuscan infantry were never as renowned as those of 12th to 13th-century Lombardy, but they survived longer and were greatly influenced by 'Saracen' infantry from Lucera, adopting some of their offensive infantry tactics as well as their short stabbing-swords, used to attack enemy cavalry.

While mercenary cavalry gradually replaced the increasingly ineffective communal cavalry, communal infantry soldiered on and defeated several foreign armies, most notably from Germany. In northern Italy, however, even infantry militias eventually degenerated into ill-trained levies like that of Antonio della Scala's Verona which was disastrously defeated in 1387. In central Italy, the Florentine militia cavalry fell into rapid decline from 1337: the crossbow militia meanwhile was strengthened, but it did not evolve into the sort of crossbow-armed, middle-class national guard seen in France. Instead the crossbowmen of Florence (and probably in other cities too) became a semi-professional corps, recruited locally from the artisan class. Most Tuscan and northern Italian cities also recruited mercenary infantry such as the famous Genoese crossbowmen or the fearsome *Almugavar* troops from Spain. The latter had evolved out of Moorish Andalusian light infantry and their tactical influence would reinforce that of the earlier 'Saracens' of Lucera.

One simple reason why local militias endured so long was the size of their numbers, which could be very large as the proportion of recruits from the sur-

'Soldiers at the Holy Sepulchre' dating from the late 13th century. (*In situ*, Basilica di Santo Stefano, Bologna)

The main square in Pistoia with the massive tower of the cathedral to the left, originally built as a watchtower. On the right is the Palazzo Pretorio, built in 1369 and decorated with carved coats-of-arms. (Author's photograph)

LEFT **A page from the mid-14th-century Choir Books of Verona cathedral, showing a light-infantry *tabulaccio*. (Mss. LLIX & MLVIII, c.22V, Biblioteca del Duomo, Verona)**

RIGHT **Another page from Verona cathedral's Choir Books, this time showing a heavy infantry *pavesare*.**

rounding *contado* increased. Unlike urban militiamen, however, the latter were 'pressed men' who served unwillingly and for little reward. It is interesting to note too that there was often one crossbowman for every ten infantrymen in these units. By the mid-14th century there were signs of discontent even amongst élite urban crossbowmen and, although this was temporarily solved by forming them into separate units while the rest of the militia fell into decline, by the late-14th century even wealthy Florence could no longer pay its crossbow élite properly. Men began to avoid training and garrison duty, insubordination was rife and the well-off paid others to take their places. Other cities faced similar problems. The threat posed by roving armies of predatory mercenaries forced Orvieto to revive its militias but they proved ineffective. In 1366 a league of central Italian cities was formed to deal with the menace of unemployed mercenary companies: each city provided an equal number of infantry militia, half of them crossbowmen, and cavalry largely recruited from the mercenary companies themselves. Meanwhile smaller states like Lucca, which lacked the money to hire sufficient mercenaries, continued to rely on citizen militias long after they were dissolved elsewhere.

Professional infantry often came from the same backgrounds as the militias and many may even have served as militiamen. During the 13th century the most famous units were 'Saracens' from Lucera, crossbowmen from Pisa, Corsica, Genoa and Liguria, and other foot soldiers from the hills of Romagna. Some served outside Italy, most notably Genoese crossbowmen in French service during the 14th century. Surviving *condotta* contracts provide details of how they were recruited, equipped and paid. Most were enlisted as groups rather than individuals, and the standardisation of arms and armour was quite surprising:

employers were usually expected to supply them with ammunition. Crossbowmen were graded according to competency: a fully qualified man was one judged capable of repairing a crossbow, while a 'master crossbowman' could make such a weapon from scratch.

Frequent tension between militia infantry and professional foot soldiers may have been the result of insecurity on the part of the militia, who rightly felt that their position was under threat. Certainly, many states were increasingly happy to collect fines instead of enforcing militia service, since the money could be used to hire professionals. It was also a 'buyer's market' with plenty of troops available. A small standing army, free from local political involvement, was the preferred option of many of those governing the cities. Many constitutions were modified to allow for this; for example, Florence drew up new legal codes in 1337 so that each *masnada* of 50 professional infantrymen had to include at least 20 non-Florentines. The unwillingness of Florentine militiamen, whether from city or *contado*, to do tedious garrison duty meant that increasing numbers of professionals were enlisted in the 1360s and 1370s. The 1378 Ciompi Revolt, led by the *Popolo Minuto* and vote-less artisans, finally put an end to the Florentine militia system, and thereafter crossbowmen were almost entirely drawn from full-time 'foreign' professional *stipendiari* who brought their families with them. Whole units were hired complete with their own support, command structures and military bands.

HOME AND WORK

Less is known about the everyday life of middle-class people in medieval Europe than is known about the experiences of the aristocracy. However, because there was a large, literate urban bourgeoisie in Italy, we know more about the Italian medieval middle class than of their European contemporaries. The idea that peasants were constantly fleeing to cities in search of a better life is an over-simplification. So is the idea that the old social order broke down in the face of new economic changes. In fact in the late-14th century the status of individuals and families did not change much, while the social hierarchy seems to have become more rigid, not less so. Those who migrated to cities from the countryside often kept close links with their original villages since kinship ties were essential for individual and family security. Meanwhile the concentration of inter-related groups within specific parts of a city increased their economic, political and military power.

Family structures changed significantly in the 11th and 12th centuries as a result of an increase in the importance of patrilineal authority. This meant that fathers had almost complete authority over their children, family, servants and retainers. There was, inevitably, a corresponding decline in

Part of the story of 'The Capture of Napo della Torre by the Milanese' late-13th-century wall-paintings. (*In situ*, Angera castle; author's photograph)

Field-fortifications of quilted fabric and timber to defend crossbowmen, in Guido da Vigevano's military treatise of 1335. (Ms. Lat. 11015, f. 41v, Bibliothèque Nationale, Paris)

Interior of the Castello Visconteo in Pavia, built by Galeazzo II between 1360–65: it is typical of the imposing fortifications preferred by the *signori*. (Author's photograph)

the status of women. This change in family life was more true of the aristocracy than of other classes in Italy. For most medieval Italian families, links with the mother's as well as the father's family remained strong. This persistence of the *consortia* in Italy meant that there was often an equal sharing of the parental inheritance. The political turmoil often witnessed in towns also strengthened the reliance on this system, particularly amongst the middle classes: it was dangerous to concentrate the family's wealth in the hands of one, vulnerable individual, and wiser to spread the risk as widely as possible. Such arrangements could be linked to 'tower societies', in which several heirs or unrelated families joined forces to build and defend fortified *torri*, a feature that came to dominate the Italian urban skyline. The *consortia* also had an outer circle of distant relatives, sometimes in other parts of the country, who served as useful business contacts or provided refuge in times of crisis. Within a few generations a *consortia* could be made up of hundreds of people and scores of branches. All the while though, the wife's rights over her husband's property were being whittled away: it was considered safer to place wealth in the hands of men strong enough to fight in its defence.

One way families defended themselves at a time when governments were rarely able to maintain law and order was by the *vendetta*. Originally the code of *vendetta* was carefully circumscribed so that it did not get out of control. Vengeance had to be '*condencens*' (appropriate) and not excessive, only involving those regarded as guilty of the original offence, and a close relative of the injured party. The man who carried out the *vendetta*, particularly if it involved killing, would take vengeance and then flee to a place where his family had relatives. The family would then be tried in his absence, and then subsequently seek reconciliation with those on the other side. This was usually possible once injuries were judged to be equal, though a guilty individual still needed to obtain a pardon from the city authorities, usually after his family had paid a fine.

A revival of Roman law in the 13th century meant that a father retained control

over his adult children until he decided to emancipate them. In many cases, children were not set free until their father died. This meant that a young man could only follow a military career if his *paterfamilia* agreed, although coercion could be used to gain paternal consent.

It is often assumed that medieval close-families were large, and that they lived in overcrowded and insanitary conditions. This was clearly not the case in Italian cities where the average 13th–14th-century family was made up of three to four people – much like the modern nuclear family. Disease, rather than war, also meant that the average age of the population remained relatively low.

Social and sexual attitudes were extremely varied in medieval Italy. Some attitudes were modern and progressive, while others now seem shocking. For example, in the 13th–14th centuries women usually married in their early teens: men however did not tend to wed until their 30s, in stark contrast to the early Middle Ages when young boys were often forced into marriage. Indeed much of the characteristic violence and unrest in Italian cities was blamed on young men who had little else to do in a segregated society. For reasons unknown, women outnumbered men by a three-to-two majority. We can only assume that the widely differing age-gap between husbands and wives hindered the development of a sense of true companionship, though romantic ideals of 'love' remained a favourite literary theme. No doubt the Black Death changed things: the catastrophe which wiped out entire families inevitably forced a strengthening of the bonds between generations, as well as that between husband and wife.

Italian urban housing of this period had more in common with Byzantium and the Islamic world than with cities north of the Alps. This was because in Italy, Greece and the Middle East, Roman cities had mostly survived along with their associated way of life. Most professional soldiers tended to live near the citadel or fortified palace, or in the *domus*, the great family house of their employers. Some cities provided accommodation for mercenaries, though this was not necessarily in the form of barracks. Militiamen lived in their own homes which were often part of their shops or workshops.

'Soldiers at the Crucifixion' taken from a late-14th-century wall-painting by Altichiero. (*In situ*, Chapel of S. Giacomo, the Basilica, Padua)

A detailed study of surviving medieval houses in Genoa has identified three main types (see the illustration on page 45 for examples). The first consisted of several houses with a continuous portico: this was probably associated with the *consortia* system, whereby an extended family lived in the building and operated several shops on the ground floor. The second type was the *casa-fondaco*, characteristic of the 13th–14th centuries, which was more like an inhabited warehouse. It had shops or storage areas beneath, and could have a fortified *torre* attached. The third type was a humbler structure which was divided into numerous apartments for poorer artisan families. Each structure was on a single floor with about 32 square metres of living space. The simplest houses of this period were made of wood: sadly none have survived.

Within their homes medieval Italian families took food very seriously. Bread was the staple food, and there was a huge variety of types, including special forms of sweetened, flavoured and decorated loaves for the religious feast days. Wine was also important and it too was very varied. Surviving *Ricordi* (books of family advice) provide details of a typical feastday meal in a prosperous though not aristocratic Italian family. The first course might include melon, salad and wine from Salerno or Greece, replaced by sweet wine in winter; the second course consisted of antipasti; the third of grilled meat with 'light' white wine; the fourth of roast meat with 'heavy' red wine; and the fifth of fruits with wines flavoured with aromatics and honey or with 'Mangiaguerra' (a special wine from the Campania region) or with sweet wine from Salerno. Though this seems elaborate today, it was seen as a 'simple' spread when compared to the highly decorated concoctions of French-style feasting. One might expect the diet of soldiers to have been much more basic, but the variety of foodstuff sent on an ordinary campaign suggests that military life was not always harsh (see the section *On Campaign*).

ORIGINS AND RECRUITMENT

All citizens owed *servitia debita*, or service to the state, a practice rooted in feudal concepts. During the 13th and 14th centuries, militia units comprised tax-paying citizens who remained liable for service from the ages of 15 to 70 in Florence, and from 20 to 60 in Siena. Crossbowmen may have been younger: the Society of Crossbowmen in Italian-influenced Ragusa (present-day Dubrovnik) were aged between 16 and 40 in the late-14th century. Although the militia did not draw men from the poorest sections of society, there were still plenty of recruits: this was because the *Popolo Minuto* formed almost 60 per cent of the population in many 14th-century cities. Once recruited, infantrymen were grouped into units which varied in size according to local conditions. The four main classes of militia were the cavalry, the heavy infantry including *pavesari*, the light infantry and the archers (including crossbowmen). The majority of rural *contadini* served as very low status pioneers or labourers.

The prejudice against archery, common throughout western Europe, meant that it took time for crossbowmen to become a military (though never a social) élite. For example, the few Florentine crossbowmen known to us include a bootmaker, a leather gilder, a dyer, a fish-monger, a baker and a tailor. Only when skill and luck enabled an individual to rise higher in society does more detailed information survive. One of the most interesting biographies preserved is that of Johannes of Fulgineo, near Arezzo. This master crossbowman, and noted marksman, was recruited by the Dalmatian maritime city of Ragusa, arriving there in 1376. His first contract was to make 20 crossbows '*da braccio*' and three '*da baloardo*' for the sum of 45 gold ducats. He made good contacts with local guild leaders and went into business with other men from Italy, Dalmatia and southern France, including a 'diver' from Ancona, a rope-maker from Venice, a smith from Zara, and an armourer from Lecce. When he was about 30 years old, Johannes married Ruchna, the 16-year-old daughter of a leading Ragusa merchant. He later purchased a vineyard and a merchant ship, and in addition received a special allowance for his services to the city.

The details of recruitment varied from place to place, but in general prosperous, middle-class immigrants were usually welcomed in the *societates armorum* (militia companies). In the far north-west, the feudal kingdom of Savoy had much in common with neighbouring France, and to the east the city state of Verona had a militia system in which duties like *guaite* (manning the walls) mirrored the French system of *guet* (urban guard duty). Crossbow militiamen played the major role in the *guaite*, whereas *decene* (garrison duty outside the city's walls) seems to have fallen to everyone. Incidentally, we also know that the Veronese militia crossbowmen were under strict instruction to maintain their weapons in good condition, and that there were normally five times as many ordinary stirrup-type *balestre a staffa* as there were larger *balestre da due piedi*.

In Florence the militia was reorganised into four quarters after 1342, each providing four units under their *gonfalonieri* officers. Each militia group (or *società*) was still supposed to include cavalry, heavy infantry and crossbowmen in the proportions of 1:2:2, but a crisis in 1354 led to an élite force of 800 crossbowmen being selected from the 16 *gonfaloni* companies and put under a *constable*. In rival Siena, the *Podestà* continued to enforce militia conscription, with each of the *contrade* (small wards or precincts) supposedly maintaining its own company. Not all men were eligible to join here. They had to be 'good and faithful *popolani*', resident in the surrounding *contado*, or foreigners who had proved their loyalty to Siena. Others were excluded because their families were involved in a *vendetta* or because they were from the aristocratic class.

Less is known about southern Italian militias, that had a comparatively minor military role to play. Yet even a small Calabrian town like Nicotera still had its own militia in the late-13th century. Over the straits in Sicily, the traditional *xurteri* (night-watch militia companies) were deemed ineffective by the early-14th century, seeing as most men found an excuse to avoid service. Instead, during a period of near anarchy when

A soldier tries to defend his lover as both are driven into Hell, on a wall-painting of the 'Inferno' by Orcagna, 1348–50. The soldier still has his shield, *bacinetto*, mail *gorgiera* and *basilarda* dagger. (Museo dell'Opera di Santa Croce, Florence; photograph by Niccolò Orso Battaglini)

23

the Aragonese rulers of Sicily had to desperately defend their cities against attack by their rival Naples, an array of *comitivi* (private armies) had sprung up and taken over this role. The loyalty of these *comitivi* could also be bought by wealthy or powerful men who used them to control what was left of the rural interior or the surrounding *contado*.

Most rural militias were rabbles of unwilling peasantry, that were too poor to equip themselves properly; however, in some places they were a more effective fighting force. Those of the Florentine *contado*, for example, were based upon the *pieve* (a group of parishes), and each had its own *vessilli* (a detachment marching behind a banner carried by a veteran from a leading local family). These and other rural militias were listed according to their *leghe*, or unit, of which there were around 53. It is possible that the urban quarters of Florence were given responsibility for the military organisation of parts of the *contado* in the mid-13th century. The demand for troops led to an increase in the quota of militiamen recruited from the *contado*, but this led to a drop in quality: this can be clearly seen in a report dated 1364 by Coppo de Medici, which paints a dismal picture.

The little city of Lucca continued to rely on both rural and urban militias, and here the *contado* was divided into sections, each of which had to supply *pavesari*, *balestieri*, and *tabulacciari*. One 14th-century record of a muster shows that the smallest unit came from Montiscaroli (11 *balestieri*, 13 *pavesari*, seven *tabulacciari*) and the largest from the Vicariate of Camporeggiane (100, 120, and 80 respectively). We know that in 1383, 36 skilled militiamen were to be provided by each area: these men were divided into three groups which served for one month at a time. However, this proved to be both unpopular and expensive, so instead money was spent on improving the fortifications, and fewer men were employed. Thus the wages of the *cerne* rural militia were reduced.

The information available regarding Siena highlights different problems. Here the rural areas included lordships which were not strictly part of the *contado*. The military obligations of these lordships were defined in their original treaties of submission to the city, or *capituli*, and mostly consisted of an agreement to supply a fixed number of infantrymen, at Siena's expense. An example of this dates from 1302, when a special force of 2,000 *contadini* was recruited from the nine vicariates of the *contado*, on the basis that their dominant families had shown traditional loyalty to Siena and the Guelf cause. Their primary function was to defend the Sienese *Popolo Grasso* and *Popolo Minuto* against attack from their own *grandi* magnates or aristocracy. Although such obligations could be demanding, they were

ABOVE **'Siena's Chamberlain and clerk at work' on the cover of the Biccherna records for the year 1388. (Archivio di Stato, Siena)**

RIGHT **Detail from a 1338–39 allegorical wall-painting by Ambroglio Lorenzetti representing 'Bad Government in the Country': here, soldiers are abducting a woman. (*In situ*, Palazzo Pubblico, Siena)**

BELOW **Fragment of a damaged early-14th-century wall-painting showing a hilltop castle and fortified village. (*In situ*, Palazzo Pubblico, Siena)**

difficult to change. To further complicate the situation, a parallel system of nine *podestarile* (police districts) was established under the authority of the *Podestà*, with differing boundaries to the nine vicariates still within the authority of the *Capitano del Popolo*.

Complicated as such systems were, the city states of Tuscany at least enjoyed effective authority over their territories. The neighbouring Papal States did not. Here, demands or even pleading requests for the various cities to send their military units were often ignored. At best it resulted in the despatch of a few cavalrymen, with a notable unwillingness to send militia cross-bowmen. In Sicily, economic collapse meant that a pool of militarily skilled manpower was available. Much of the interior of the island was now inhabited by just a small number of semi-nomadic pig farmers and brigands, and here the ordinary people were noted for their hunting skills. Crossbows as well as composite hand-bows, javelins and spears were all used during wide-ranging boar-hunts which resembled military expeditions. More modest though equally exotic sources of militiamen and mercenaries were the overseas colonial outposts of Venice and Genoa.

Mercenary infantrymen were not necessarily full-time professionals. Most seem to have come from upland or mountainous regions of Italy. Over-population in the Alps and northern Apennines meant that soldiering became a secondary occupation for much of the rural population. They were also regarded as being different to the inhabitants of the cities: independent-minded, physically strong, impulsive and aggressive but poor, they were in fact ideal military material. Those in command of mercenary infantry units were usually Italian, whereas cavalry leaders recruited a large number of non-Italians into their ranks. Sources show that many officers commanding Genoese crossbowmen in 14th-century France were highly experienced. For example, a certain Conrart Grimaldi served from 1370 to 1395, and had fought in Italy in 1369: also, Odet d'Ansart, a *constable* in command of 19 mounted crossbowmen, was a 'squire from the territory of Genoa' whose coat-of-arms consisted of a chevron and two stars *en chef*, a crossbow *en pointe* and a *champ festonné*, marked with a bundle of arrows. Some officers came from the noble families of Spinola, Doria and Grimaldi: others were known in the simple form of 'Martin of Parma', 'Guy of Pisa', 'Francis of Naples' or 'Anthony of Piacenza'.

BELOW **Another detail from Lorenzetti's 'Bad Government in the Country': here soldiers are depicted leaving a city.**

'Guards at the Court of Justice' in a manuscript from Bologna made *c.* 1356. (Cod. 2048, f. 149r, Österreichische Nationalbibliothek, Vienna)

BELOW **A scene from 'The Execution of St. James and his companions' on a silver altar panel made by Leonardo di Ser Giovanni in 1371. (*In situ*, Pistoia cathedral; author's photograph)**

Men who served as militiamen might seek employment as mercenaries elsewhere if their hometown was not at war. Many were recruited within their own cities by agents for an employer elsewhere. Feudal barons from Naples, Rome, the Romagna and Lombardy similarly offered entire units of their own followers to friendly cities: these men were then paid by the city and were not strictly mercenaries. Cities would lend militia to their allies too. In addition, individual travellers would recruit soldiers for protection, particularly in the middle and later 14th century when banditry reached epidemic proportions. Some of those hired had however been bandits themselves, and would return to it when no better-paid employment could be found.

A surviving Genoese contract dated 13 April 1254 states that Giordano the Crossbowman recruited Giovanni the Crossbowman for 29 weeks, as well as Ughetto the Crossbowman, who was to replace the late Aimerico of Barbagetala. Most of these men came from the coastal mountains of Liguria rather than Genoa itself, though the city remained the centre of recruitment. Other so-called 'Genoese' crossbowmen came from far away. A list of these men in French service in 1378 shows that it was led by Guy of Pisa, and consisted of William, Anthony and Hugh from Pisa, Antony from Lucca, Antony from Venice, Mas from Messina, Richard from Naples, as well as many non-Italians. Among the Italians commanded by Antoide Quinaille that same year were Daniel and Peter from Venice, Bernard from Monaco, John from Modena and Antony from Sicily.

Piedmont and Savoy were a further source of infantry. The troops from the Val d'Aosta were regarded as experts in mountain siege warfare. Also, crossbowmen from Mantua served in many locations, infantry from Lucca's *contado* took service under foreign flags, and foot soldiers from San Bancrazio appeared in late-13th-century Florentine army lists. In the latter, we also know that Catalan mercenaries were replaced by men from France and southern Italy in 1314–15. Men from Spoleto served in Siena, where a three-man commission called the Lords of the *Masnada* monitored mercenary performance, the best being rewarded with bonus pay. By the mid-13th century, a large part of the Papal army consisted of Tuscan infantry. Italian professional infantry could also find themselves being sent on crusade, as in 1366 when Gian Galeazzo Visconti of Milan recruited 300 *brigandi*, mostly from Genoa, then 'loaned' them to the Count of Savoy who sailed off to capture Gallipoli in Turkey. These *brigandi* garrisoned the city, but were carefully watched by the suspicious Savoyard nobles: numerous pirate fleets were roaming the Aegean and Black Seas at this point, containing a large number of Italians in their ranks, and were no doubt on the look-out for eager new recruits.

The command structure of Italian infantry militias was simple. In late-13th-century Padua, the *Podestà* presented standards to each of the *gastaldiones* (leaders of the guild militias): the banner of the *Podestà* was held by an officer called the *iudex ancianorum*. In Lucca the four *gonfalonieri* militia commanders each had four *pennonieri* (junior officers) responsible for looking after banners and summoning the men. These officers were elected either by the General Council of Lucca or by a smaller executive committee called the Thirty-Six. The role of *gonfaloniere* could not pass directly from father to son, or from brother to brother, except after a four-month interval. In Florence each militia unit was led by a *gonfalonierius*, supported by two

The cathedral and baptistry of Pisa, seen from the Leaning Tower in 1958, before the city spread much beyond its medieval walls. The open area around these buildings was used for militia training. (Author's photograph)

distringitori (explainers) and a *consigliere* ('consul' or representative). The commander of an archer or crossbow unit here was called a *bandifer*; also, the *pavesari* were divided into three *vexilla* units. In Siena the *Capitano del Popolo* and *Podestà* shared responsibility for militia units, along with a 'war captain', a post created early in the 14th century. Sienese militia companies were headed by a captain with a standard bearer and three councillors, all at least 30 years old and selected from 'men of property' within that particular quarter of the city. Each captain swore loyalty to the Guelf party and the city of Siena, and every man in the company might also have to swear the same, to ensure that no hated Ghibelline entered their ranks. In 1310 Siena decided that only citizens should command rural militia units, as opposed to the *Podestà*'s 'foreign' assistants, who were instead given the role of rural police officers. However, as the Italian militia system fell apart in the 1390s, officers were mostly drawn from the old feudal élite, and were almost all 'foreign' mercenaries in so far as they came from other parts of Italy.

PAY AND MOTIVATION

Several different currencies were used in 13th–14th-century Italy, while inflation was as prominent though not as drastic as in the present day. In early-14th-century Siena, records show that each militia company had its own notary or clerk who served as treasurer: so many captains had embezzled company funds that such appointments were considered vital. The funds available covered the renting of store-rooms as well as paying the men. Two copies of the account books were kept, listing members: one remained with the notary, and the other was kept by the company captain. Both men had to show their records to the *Podestà*, the *Capitano del Popolo* and the city courts on request.

Clearly the high pay offered to some 13th-century crossbowmen was dependent upon their attaining a certain level of skill. In general, there is evidence of an overall rise in military salaries in the 13th century, particularly in the rich city-states. Wages naturally increased in times of crisis. In 1282 King Charles of Naples offered twelve gold tari a month (a handsome sum) to crossbowmen and spearmen, while elsewhere pay appeared more modest. In 1260 the Florentine army gave three shillings a day to crossbowmen, two shillings and eight pence to ordinary archers, two shillings and six pence to *pavesari*, two shillings to ordinary infantry, and a mere shilling to sappers or pioneers. Such figures considered on their own appear almost meaningless, but do provide a useful indication of comparative pay-rates. Almost everywhere crossbowmen were paid more than *pavesari*, while cavalry received considerably more than both of these. For example, during the war between Florence and Pistoia in 1302, horsemen received nine florins a month, while the crossbowmen were paid only one florin, despite being described as 'specialists'. Garrison duty on an exposed frontier could guarantee an increase in pay, while service in dangerous wooden *battifolle* towers during a siege might result in a bonus.

Officers were naturally paid more than their men: in Piedmont in 1286 a crossbowman received three florins a month, rising to four by 1288, whereas a captain of crossbowmen in 1266 already received five florins monthly. Elsewhere, surviving plans drawn up for an early-14th-century crusade suggest that knights should receive four times the pay of a crossbowman. In peacetime the *constabli* of Florence were given 40 soldi per month, while their men received only 25: in time of war, this was increased to six and three florins respectively. The rewards that a 'master crossbowman' could expect were higher still: by the late-14th century, their pay was sometimes higher than that of a cuirass-maker.

Other useful sources of income were booty (of special import on naval expeditions) and the ransom extracted from captured enemies. We know for example that at Vercelli in 1232, 20 soldi were offered for cavalry prisoners, and 15 for infantry. We also know that in 1318 the Sienese militia rioted because they were stopped from sacking Massa following its surrender, which goes to show just how strongly the troops felt about this. Governments, not surprisingly, often encouraged these income supplements, since military expenditure could consume over a third of the state's revenues. But money was not the only motivation: religion also played a part. For example Ghibelline opposition to the Pope and his Guelf supporters was to some extent a rejection of the Papacy's authority, particularly his claim to temporal authority. Similarly, those fighting in support of the Pope during the Italian crusades often wore crosses sewn to the left shoulder. Many Italians though found these so-called crusades distasteful, and the friars preaching them had to be protected by military escorts.

However, loyalty to the local city-state was by far the strongest motivation to fight. According to

Detail from Ambroglio Lorenzetti's 1338–39 allegorical wall-painting representing 'Good Government in the Country', showing hunting with crossbows. (*In situ*, Palazzo Pubblico, Siena)

Two men wrestling outside a castle. Wrestling played an important part in military training. (*In situ*, Avio castle; author's photograph)

the Florentine chronicler Giovanni Villani; 'the lordly pride of the Primo Popolo and our ancestors was inspired by the pomp of the *carroccio* and the *marinella*'. Many cities had such a *carroccio* ceremonial wagon as a focus of civic identity. In Siena, for example, cavalry swore allegiance to the communal banner while infantry militia swore upon the *carroccio*. Tension between various quarters within a city and between economic classes or rival families frequently resulted in violence, but communal solidarity and obedience to elected representatives remained strong.

While codes of chivalry put some brake on the horrors of war elsewhere in Europe, Italian militias often had little respect for them: non-noble troops were usually outside the protection offered by such codes. Knights were happy to slaughter the militia, so they were happy to slaughter knights, except when the latter generated handsome ransoms. Outside the southern kingdoms of Naples and Sicily, the remnants of chivalry gradually withered away. However, it is interesting to note how in 14th-century Sicily a peculiar parody of chivalry emerged, where leaders of the *comitivo* armed gangs used pomp and almost heraldic dress to threaten and impress rivals, and to attract recruits.

Unit solidarity within the militias was based upon other real or imagined traditions. Genoese crossbowmen, for example, formed a corporation whose traditions governed behaviour, professional standards and mutual support. The identity provided by banners and military music also served to reinforce the sense of cohesion within each unit. Italian heraldry often disregarded the rules as understood north of the Alps, and had its own way of doing things. For example, the city militias often tried to restrict the colours used on their flags to those appearing on the city's banner. Colour could also be manipulated for political ends. The red and white arms of the Primo Popolo republican government in Florence were a symbolic inversion of the white and red used by the previous regime: a white lily on a red background became a red lily on a white background. One unit of troops defending the Florentine *carroccio* had a small red cross on a white background while the second unit used this colour scheme reversed. Florentine militia crossbowmen also had two flags, each marked with a crossbow but with the colours reversed. Comparable flags for the *pavesari* and the handbow archers also followed this practice. The near uniform armament and colour scheme of militia units also had a big impact on battlefield morale.

The quarters of a city could have entirely separate coats-of-arms unrelated to that of the city itself. Guild banners often portrayed something to do with that guild's craft or business. A separate system of militia flags might have a deep-rooted explanation from the past: for example, when the *Popolo* government reorganised the Florentine militias into twenty *gonfaloni* in the mid-13th century, each had its own distinctive insignia which was put on its flag, the shields and sometimes its helmets. All of this helped forge a sense of unity among the units during a time of crisis.

Italian militia armies were more disciplined than most of their European contemporaries, yet sanctions were still needed to maintain high standards. In Florence in the 1260s, large fines were imposed for failure to attend muster while smaller fines were imposed for not having the proper kit. In Lucca a man who was ill had to send a substitute. In Siena a man who failed to hurry, fully armed, to muster in times of '*Rumor*' (disquiet) paid a hefty fine: if he failed to pay on time, he had a foot amputated. Fines for men who could not be caught were imposed on their community instead. Penalties for officers who failed in their duties were even higher. Nevertheless only strong governments could impose such sanctions.

TACTICS AND TRAINING

Medieval infantry tactics were quite simple. Nevertheless centuries of Byzantine and Islamic military influence meant that Italian foot soldiers operated in a more complex manner than those north of the Alps. Communal militias were trained to fight in ranks in front of their *carroccio*, often behind ditches and field fortifications: their primary role was to resist enemy cavalry and enable their own horsemen to counter-attack.

In Tuscany, these tactics had been refined by the late-13th century: the *pavesari* now formed a wall with their two-metre-high rectangular shields, protecting the spearmen and crossbowmen behind. The mid-13th to early-14th centuries marked the high point of *balestieri–pavesari* team-tactics, and as a result *pavesari* could transform their unit into a kind of moving fortress, fending off the enemy with their *lanzelonghe* spears while the protected crossbowmen maintained a steady rate of fire. This was an advance on the old Romano-Byzantine *testudo* moving 'fortress' of shields, and the protection afforded by the *pavesari* enabled the crossbowmen to make full use of their weapons' accuracy. Its limited speed however permitted the more heavily armoured cavalry to regain the tactical initiative.

This *balestieri–pavesari* collaboration was not as tactically successful as the unit organisation of the 'Saracens' of Lucera. Their combined use of composite bows, crossbows and javelins enabled them to maintain a significantly higher rate of fire, while their greater agility permitted offensive manoeuvres even against cavalry. It took time for 'offensive' light infantry to make a significant

'November' in the series of wall-paintings representing 'The Labours of the Months', dating from *c.* 1400. Late autumn was the main season for hunting. (*In situ*, Castello del Buonconsiglio, Trento; author's photograph)

return to the Italian battlefield, though during the 14th century Italian foot soldiers continued to play a major role in conflicts in mountainous or hilly regions. In mid-14th-century Savoy, for example, the *brigandi* were grouped into *banderie* units of 25 crossbowmen or 25 *pavesari*. Their methods of coordination and cooperation in battle are unknown. Elsewhere it seems that existing militia formations had become too large and unwieldy. We know that in Florence in 1356 an élite of 4,000 crossbowmen – all 'proven men' – were re-formed into special units. Elsewhere surviving lists of equipment for selected infantry forces indicate the role they were expected to play. For example, the Statutes of Lucca from 1372 state that the *constable*'s élite crossbowmen must have a *corazzina* or *lorica* armour, a helmet, dagger, sword, crossbow, a *faretra pro pilloctis* (special quiver), and a *crocco* (hook) to span the weapon, whereas the equipment required for ordinary crossbowmen was merely a *capo* (helmet), dagger, crossbow, ordinary quiver, and a *crocco*.

'Pope Boniface crowned at Anagni while his enemies are driven out', depicted in the early-14th-century *Croniche* of Giovanni Villani. (Cod. Chigi. VIII, 296, f. 176r, Biblioteca Apostolica Vaticana, Rome)

Disciplined infantry tactics and use of the crossbow required regular training and in 1162 Pisa introduced a law obliging citizens to practise with the crossbow, spear and 'Sardinian javelin'. More importantly, unit training instilled confidence in the face of an attack, while also maintaining a steady supply of adequately skilled and able crossbowmen. From the late-11th century onwards several urban militias seem to have trained weekly in an infantry counterpart to the better-known knightly tournament. The emphasis was clearly on discipline, as well as on the ability to move as a unit and to withstand a cavalry charge. Experience of the latter was provided by militia cavalry who 'attacked' their infantry colleagues in open spaces in front of churches, outside city walls, on main roads, or on a specially designated *campo de batalia* (battlefield). In Bergamo in 1179 one particular training exercise is referred to as a 'battle with small shields' which suggests light infantry training: this became more common during the 13th century. All classes took part in what became a form of public entertainment. Wooden weapons were used in these *pugne* or 'fights': we also know that judges imposed heavy fines on anybody caught using iron weapons. By the 14th century such exercises often degenerated into brawls in which only youngsters took part: this in itself reflected the decline of the urban militias.

Detail from an early-14th-century wall-painting by Guidoriccio da Fogliano showing an army encampment. Senior officers have large tents while the ordinary militia live in grass huts. (*In situ*, Palazzo Pubblico, Siena)

Practice with the crossbow was a more individual affair, though it took place in areas set aside by the ruling bodies. There were also competitions which, like the one instituted in Pisa in 1286, drew in competitors and organised teams from other cities. In 1295 Venice tried to ban all games except crossbow shooting at various *bersagli* (butts) in and around the city, where all men between the ages of

15 and 35 were supposed to practise. In 1349 the Genoese government established an extensive training area outside the Olivella Gate, to be known as the '*terra de arcubus*'. During the crisis of 1354 Florence insisted on militiamen practising regularly, with a decorated crossbow being given to the champion marksman: also, in both city and *contado*, religious feast days were often marked by shooting competitions.

ABOVE **A page from the late-14th-century *Croniche del Codice Lucchese* by Sercambi, showing militia rooting out bandits.**

BELOW **Another page from the *Croniche del Codice Lucchese*, detailing the erection of field-fortifications outside Ineba. (Archivio di Stato, Lucca)**

ON CAMPAIGN

The command structure of communal armies differed from that of feudal forces. In the latter authority was usually based upon age and social status. In communal forces command was more varied, and although members of the aristocracy usually still held positions of authority, this reflected their experience and military reputation rather than mere noble status. Strategic decisions were made by those who ruled the city, though such men were usually aware of their limited military knowledge and so delegated immediate command to a professional. The latter tended to be 'foreigners': the idea was that as outsiders they were above factionalism, which was a characteristic feature of Italian cities of this period. For example, on campaign the Florentine *Podestà* was assisted by a council of twelve captains, two from each *sesto* (or city-quarter). He was also permitted to strike disobedient men – a great privilege at a time when personal affront and injury could lead to an immediate *vendetta*. The *Podestà* was not supposed to take part in the fighting though: instead he directed operations from behind the line.

By the second half of the 13th century most Italian

Genoese *pavesari* training, *c.* 1260

A

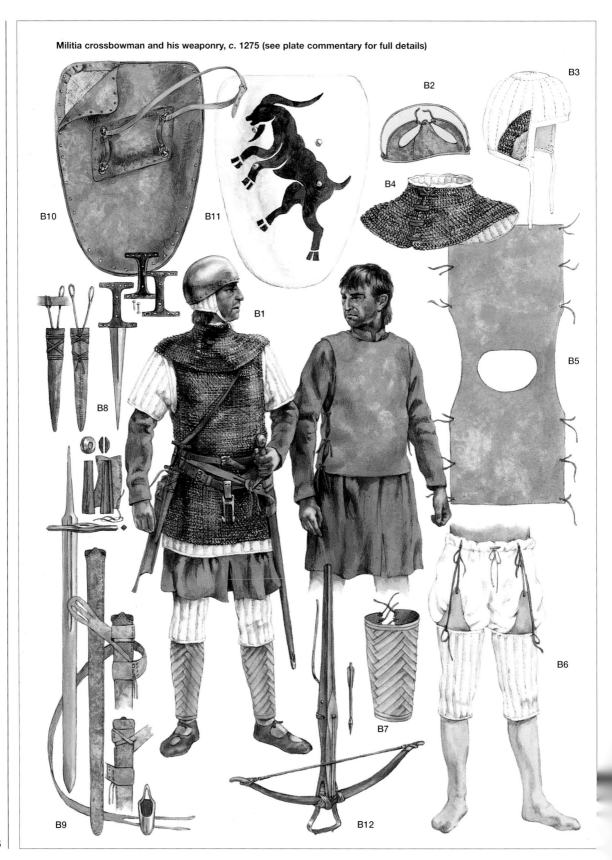

Militia crossbowman and his weaponry, c. 1275 (see plate commentary for full details)

B1 B2 B3 B4 B5 B6 B7 B8 B9 B10 B11 B12

B

The Battle of Campaldino, 1289

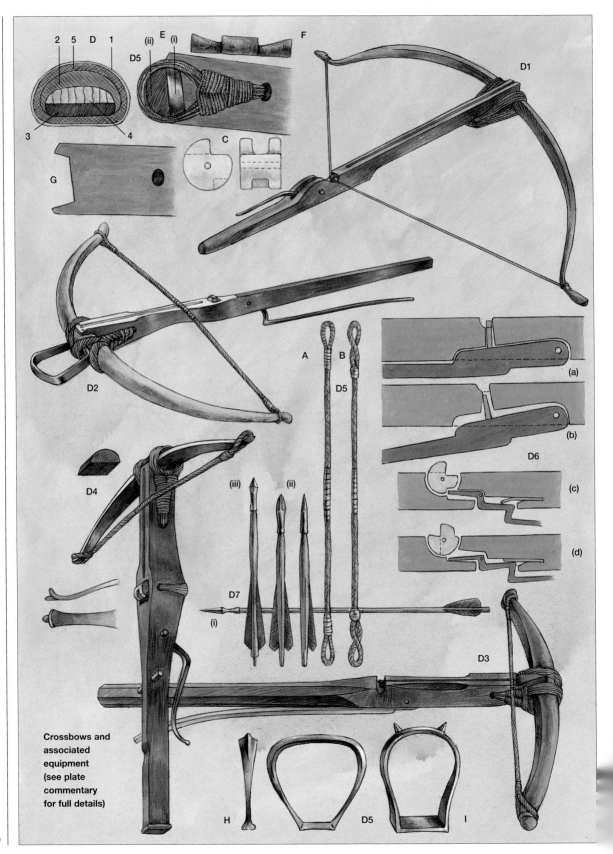

Crossbows and
associated
equipment
(see plate
commentary
for full details)

D

E2
E1
E7
E12
E8
E16
E11
E4
E15
E9
E10
E13
E3
E14
E17
E20
E19
E5
E6
E18

Crossbow spanning systems
(see plate commentary
for full details)

E

Militiaman of Lucca summoned from his shop, c. 1310

F

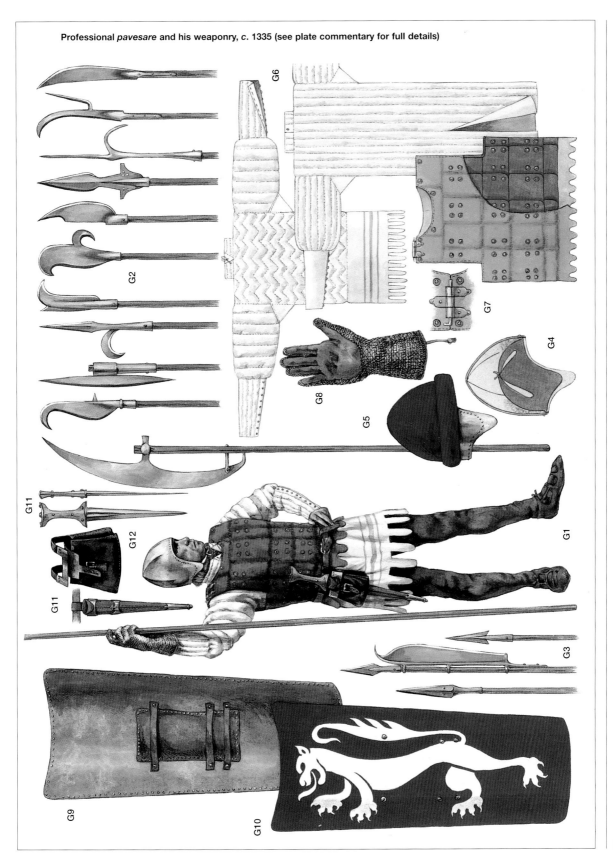

Professional *pavesare* and his weaponry, *c.* 1335 (see plate commentary for full details)

G

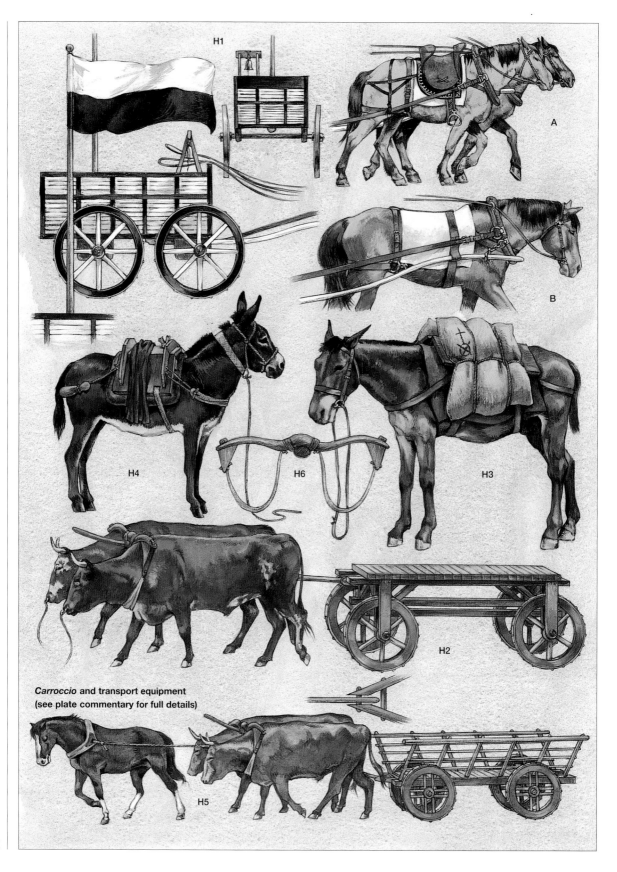

H1

A

B

H4

H6

H3

H2

Carroccio and transport equipment
(see plate commentary for full details)

H5

H

Urban warfare in the Adige Valley, *c.* 1345

Light infantry *spadaccino* in Papal service, *c.* 1375 (see plate commentary for full details)

J3

J2

J7

J8

J6

J1

J5

2

4

J4

3

1

J

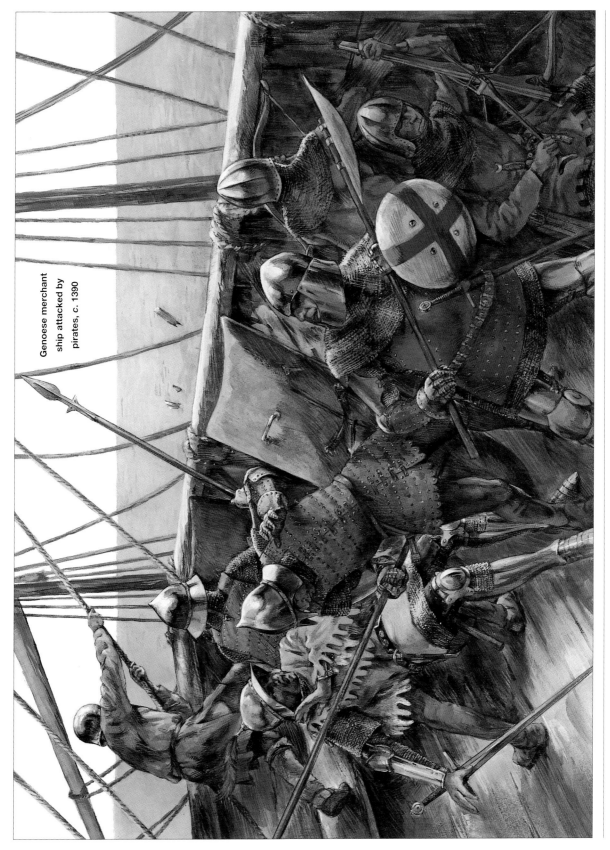

Genoese merchant ship attacked by pirates, c. 1390

K

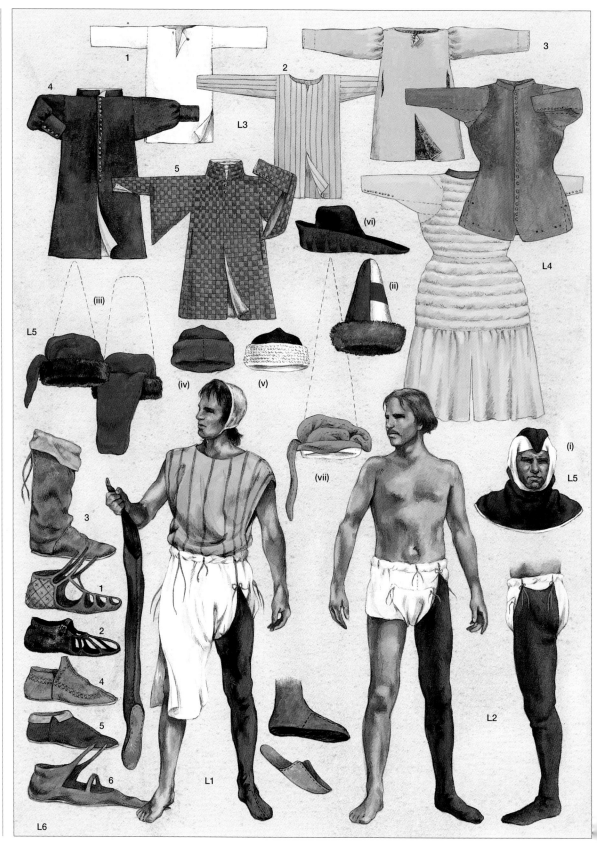

Non-military clothing (see plate commentary for full details)

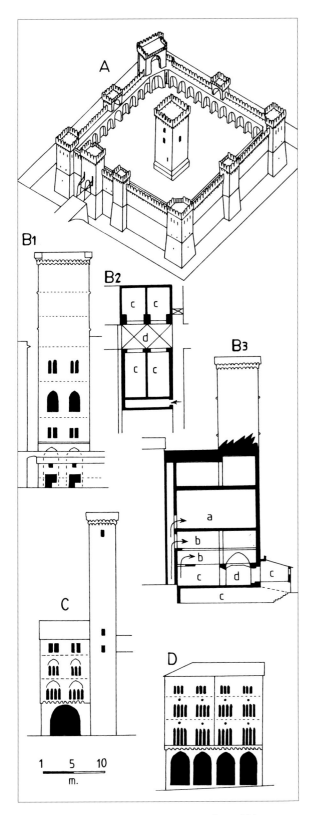

warfare was a matter of manoeuvre, raiding and sieges, with few pitched battles. This often entailed prolonged campaigns where professionals were more effective than part-time militias. In 14th-century Florence, for example, militia service obligations usually only lasted from ten to fourteen days. Even so it was rare for more than a third of the militia to be called up at one time. Instead of summoning all those from one quarter, a proportion would be taken from each, the aim being to avoid disrupting economic life.

Tactical units varied in size according to circumstance, but the *venticinquina* (or 25-man unit) was one of the most widely employed. Another interesting feature was the habit of forming tactical units of men from similar trades or occupations, presumably to strengthen comradeship and morale. The smiths, physicians and musicians who accompanied these armies on campaign would also have helped maintain both the fighting effectiveness and the morale of the troops. Crossbowmen were generally brigaded separately from the other infantry, as were the *guastatori* and the 'army market' which accompanied the troops. The late-13th-century Florentine baggage train was divided into two sections, each with a special guard unit under its own officer: one defended the vital *carroccio*, the other protected the camp followers.

On the march, Italian armies tended to follow the advice of the late-Roman military author Vegatius, with light infantry and light cavalry defending the baggage train. In enemy territory archers and crossbowmen would be placed at the head of the column, the *carroccio* in the centre with cavalry in the rear. Wagons provided the main form of military transport: this is not surprising, given that more of the old Roman road system had survived in Italy than in most other parts of western Europe, and that during the 14th century the Italian city states paved their major trade routes. Wagons came in several shapes and sizes, but in hilly areas mules and donkeys were used instead. Pack-horses or *ronzini* were differentiated from the far more expensive war-horses, and were forcibly 'borrowed' from the citizens.

Despite a tendency to conduct longer and longer campaigns, most remained limited in both scope and in the number of men involved. In a

A: the castle of Imola, east of Bologna, as it would have appeared in the early 14th century. B1–B3: a tower house in Genoa (a – main hall; b – middle rooms; c – shops; d – undercroft). C: Casa Maruffo in Genoa, a house with a tower attached. D: Case Gattilusio in Genoa, a pair of houses built in 1310.

republic, all operations had to be agreed by a city's Grand Council, which decided upon the command structure to be adopted. Those on the receiving end of raids often attempted to ambush the enemy on the march, either using an élite cavalry force in open country or infantry if the enemy was hit in hills or mountains. Armies were similarly exposed and vulnerable while assembling at a designated campsite.

A typical example of a small-scale campaign can be found in the one launched by Perugia against Foligno in June 1282: although both formed part of the Papal States, they were rivals. Both cities had built and garrisoned castles in an effort to control commercially important access to the sea. Though brief, this was a serious affair, as demonstrated by the fact that the entire financial resources of Perugia were dedicated to the campaign. The *comune* also procured and distributed arms, demanding supplies of crossbows from its *contado* for the new castles, while merchants and artisans all had to supply certain articles from a list carefully composed by the authorities. In addition, the *comune* organised the distribution of food and military supplies to the zone of operations, with two officials called *superstites* checking movements in and out of every city gate. Economic warfare was after all just as important as military action.

The cavalry may have once more come to dominate the battlefield by the second half of the 14th century, but the infantry militia could still demonstrate its effectiveness and importance at crucial moments. For example, when Florence determined to block the passage of the infamous Grand Company of mercenaries across the Apennines in July 1356, it was the 2,500 crossbowmen sent to man the passes that forced the unwelcome visitors to turn back. The same 'impasse' resulted the following year, but in 1358 Florence gave the Grand Company permission to continue its journey to Siena. In the Scalella Valley, however, 12,000 local mountain folk decided that the mercenaries were causing too much damage and attacked them. The battered survivors eventually negotiated their safe passage out of Florentine territory.

Byzantine-Roman and Middle Eastern influence is clearly evident in the careful arrangement of medieval Italian military encampments, as well as in the bureaucratic inspections of troops and horses by marshals upon arrival there. This ensured that items 'lost' on campaign and due for replacement by the government did actually exist in the first place, and were not merely invented. Italian field-fortifications however do not seem to have changed a great deal since the fall of the western Roman Empire: the only innovation it seems was the highly effective use of crossbows to defend them. In fact, from the 13th to the 15th century, field-fortifications (along with the tactics of siege) came to dominate Italian warfare: as a result luring an enemy out of his defences became a major priority. A revival of offensive light infantry towards the end of the 14th century may also have reflected this state of affairs, as might a short

TOP **Infantry soldiers in Altichiero's late-14th-century wall-painting 'The Martyrdom of St. Catherine'. (*In situ*, Oratorio di San Giorgio, Padua)**

ABOVE **Altichiero's 'Martyrdom of St. George', showing infantry soldiers. (*In situ*, Oratorio di San Giorgio, Padua)**

lived 13th-century experiment using 'armoured' *pantera* (light wooden wagons) to strengthen the defences. Some were even said to have light siege engines on board.

It is interesting to note that there was a dramatic increase in the intensity and effectiveness of Italian siege warfare in the 13th century when archers were largely replaced by cross-bowmen. This obliged garrisons to adopt heavier armour while fortifications themselves became more sophisticated. New fortified towns, *bastita* stockaded villages and castles sprung up along frontiers, major roads, river crossings and the junctions of important routes, in order to discourage and hinder enemy raiding. Infantrymen naturally played the dominant role when defending in siege warfare. Nevertheless it was rare for a direct assault to be made against the walls and, as in most other parts of Europe, blockades or mining were more effective than even the largest stone-throwing mangonels. Urban warfare was a more distinctive aspect of this period. During the 13th century this tended to be focused around *torri* with rival groups fighting from behind barricades, advancing from street to street and using siege machines. Rival factions would also put great effort into gaining control of the area immediately around their *torre*, either through purchase or by threats. During the 14th century, however, the importance of such *torri* declined.

The Siena army at the Battle of Val di Chiana on a wall-painting by Lippo Vanni, c. 1373. Behind the cavalry come the musicians, followed by *pavesari* and crossbowmen, with a few mounted officers. (*In situ*, Palazzo Pubblico, Siena; author's photograph)

As literacy spread, many military treatises were written and circulated. The Florentine scholar Bono Giamboni translated the famous late-Roman work by Vegatius into his local dialect in the late-13th or early-14th century, updating it to include the new infantry crossbow. Guido da Vigevani wrote his *Texaurus* in 1335, supposedly to help prepare a crusade which never actually took place. He wrote in Latin, but had to use Italian vernacular terms when referring to modern arms, armour and mechnical devices. Similar military matters preoccupied Aegidius Columna and Marino Sanudo, both of whom focused on siege warfare. Guido's ideas were the most practical however, including methods of protecting crossbowmen with quilted and seemingly fireproofed screens, a direct adoption from Arab-Islamic military technology.

Garrison duty may have been tedious, but it still had to be properly organised. Hence urban governments put considerable effort into ensuring that militiamen could get to the walls without delay or obstruction. Each unit was expected to rally around its standard-bearer at a pre-arranged spot, and then fulfil a designated duty or defend a specified section of the walls. Generally speaking, crossbowmen were assigned the crucial role of protecting the gates. In some areas the manning of outlying castles fell to rural militias who tended however to slope back to their civilian tasks unless closely supervised.

If the Italian middle classes enjoyed their food while at home, there is strong evidence that the armies also expected to be well fed. Once again, the sadly now-destroyed Neapolitan archives provided some fascinating details on this subject. In 1282, for example, the garrison of the Castel dell'Uovo in Naples consumed 300 sacks of corn, 300 *salme* of millet (one *salme* was equivalent to eight barrels), 150 salted pigs and 1,000 cheeses. In 1282, 1283 and 1284 King Charles sent the following supplies to his armies in Calabria and Sicily: boxes of biscuit (mostly consumed by naval crews), ground flour stored in large amphorae, barley, wheat, oil, millet, vegetables, vinegar, cheese, salted meat (including halves of salted pork, shoulders of ham, and thighs of ham), mutton, *capicolli* (a kind of salami), salted eels, salted carp, lard, beans, almonds, loaves of sugar, pepper, cinnamon, cloves, saffron, nutmeg, pimientos, Latin wine, Greek wine, Italian wine from Nocera, Sorrento, Castellamare di Stabia and nearby areas, herbs for medicinal purposes, twists of wax, small candles, unworked wax, horseshoes, discs to make wooden tubs, and livestock too, including two- to three-year-old live sows as well as bulls and cows.

BATTLE AND AFTERMATH

On those rare occasions when the militia risked a set-piece battle, the principal problem they faced was the physical and psychological impact of the enemy's cavalry charge. The infantry's ability to withstand such an assault was often the deciding factor in the outcome of a battle. The victories won by communal militias before the mid-13th century however had been a triumph of defence over offence:

Battle scene at Avio castle, showing light-infantrymen with small shields. (*In situ*, Avio castle; author's photograph)

they also precipitated a 'stand-off' between old and new kinds of warfare. Large battles might have been less common after 1250, but the numbers of men involved seem to have been greater and the resultant struggles longer-lasting. This was summed up in a speech by a Florentine commander before the Battle of Campaldino in 1289: 'Wars in Tuscany up till now have been won by short and sharp assaults which did not last long, and few men have been killed in them. This is all changed now. The side which stands

fast is the side which shall win.' Crossbowmen proved though that they could break the static ranks of infantry, as demonstrated by the Ghibelline leader Guido Novello near Faenza in June 1275. Later 13th- and 14th-century Tuscan infantry also often adopted a concave formation to restrict the room available to the enemy for launching a cavalry attack.

Some of the major infantry battles fought in Italy serve as examplary models. Montaperti in 1260 has been described as typifying the transitional phase between static Lombard militia tactics and fully developed Tuscan ones. Certainly the Florentine infantry remained on the defensive with only 300 *pavesari* protecting 1,000 crossbowmen, only to be defeated later when abandoned by their own cavalry. Florence's victory over Arezzo at Campaldino in 1289 involved a larger proportion of cavalry than at Montaperti while the infantry were more carefully selected. Both armies faced each other in a valley, the Florentines having their best cavalry in the centre with infantry behind and on each flank plus crossbowmen ahead of the line. To the rear the Florentine baggage train established a semi-fortified position protected by additional cavalry and unreliable allies from Lucca and Pistoia. The army of Arezzo was more innovative, though ultimately unsuccessful, through having the light infantry and cavalry charge the Florentine line together. The light infantry wrought havoc amongst the Florentine cavalry, but the Florentine reserves held off the assault and ensured a successful counter-attack. Pisa's defeat of Lucca at Montecattini in 1315 was an example of heavy infantry *pavesari* resisting an initial cavalry charge, then being broken up by Pisan crossbowmen, before finally succumbing to a further cavalry attack. Ten years later the Florentine militia were defeated by Castruccio Castracani of Lucca at the Battle of Altopascio, where a somewhat desperate *levée en masse* from the city and *contado* consisted of spearmen with inadequate numbers of crossbowmen. This composite force was crushed, in the last major battle where the Florentine militia played a dominant role.

Battle scene at Avio castle. A crossbowman is seen shooting from behind spear-armed men, who could be *scuderi*. (*In situ*, Avio castle; author's photograph)

As infantry tactics developed, so did the use of weapons. Certain characteristics of the crossbow affected the way in which it was used: most obviously, the fact that the weapon had to be held laterally meant that crossbowmen could not form such close ranks as ordinary archers. The crossbow's relatively slow rate of fire and the fact that it was shot horizontally also meant that it was more suited to shooting from a concealed position. Ranks could shoot concentrated volleys but then had to simultaneously reload, most probably while another rank stepped forward and shot. When facing English long-bowmen during the Hundred Years War, Genoese crossbowmen found that their *pavese* shields gave inadequate protection against showers of arrows falling at a steep angle. On the other hand, the English reliance on a thicket of sharpened stakes for protection would have made them vulnerable if the Genoese had been able to bring their weapons to bear. A further disadvantage of the crossbow was the impossibility of quickly removing and replacing the bowstring to protect it from rain, since special equipment was required to restring the short, thick bow.

The aftermath of battle could be appalling. At the start of this period, crossbowmen were still seen as a threat to the proper order of society, and those captured by Milan in 1246 were mutilated so that they could no longer shoot. Medical science may have been more advanced in Italy than elsewhere in western Europe, but it was still rudimentary. Priests, it was said, stood in the *carroccio*, helping the injured and ministering to the dying. Wounds from arrows and crossbow bolts were already important enough for the famous 12th-century physician Guido of Arezzo to include them in his book on *Chirurgia* (surgery). This included advice on how to remove an arrow from a man's head. First, the doctor assessed the angle of penetration, then gently loosened the arrow: where possible a small metal borer enlarged the entry hole. Removing arrows from other parts of the body involved the use of forceps to bend the barbs closer to the shaft, or placing a brass tube or goose quill over the barbs to stop them snagging on the edges of the wound. In some places such treatment, without anaesthetic of course, was provided free to men injured on campaign. Similarly their ransoms would be paid if their families could not afford to. In Siena, those in the service of the *comune* who were so badly wounded that they could no longer earn a living, were provided for in the public hospital of Santa Maria della Scala for life.

The fortified Ponte di Torri aqueduct brought water to the citadel of Spoleto. 230 metres long and 80 metres high, it was built for Cardinal Albornoz in the mid-14th century. (Author's photograph)

ARMS MANUFACTURE, TRADE AND PURCHASE

During the 12th and 13th centuries Italian arms and armour were virtually identical to those of the rest of western Europe, a result largely of the widespread arms trade and the mobility of the military élite. From the late-13th century onwards western European armourers built upon existing traditions as well as Islamic and Mongol influences to develop new forms of both protective armour and weaponry. A willingness to experiment with different materials was particularly characteristic of Italy, Germany and the Iberian peninsula. In Italy, for example, there was a significant increase in the use of quilted soft-armours, *cuir-bouilli* hardened-leather, and leather in combination with other materials. The process of manufacturing *cuir-bouilli* involved soaking the leather in cold water, then shaping it in wooden moulds before preserving, stiffening and waterproofing it with molten wax. Smaller pieces of armour were also made of vegetable-tanned cattle hide, untanned or partially dressed rawhide, or buff leather. The leather covering of wooden shields was sometimes secured with a form of cheese-paste glue.

Munitions technology required artisans with specialist skills, and these were often grouped into guilds. Within Italy several centres of arms production emerged, some of which may already have been manufacturing armaments throughout the undocumented early Middle Ages. The most important was Milan which soon exported widely. Genoa similarly had an armaments industry with the *ferrari* (iron-workers) being the second largest group of artisans in the city: the city's fame as a source of armaments though probably reflected its role as a trading port. In north-eastern Italy the metalworkers of Venice were subdivided into separate guilds of *fabbri* (general smiths), and *spadari* (swordsmiths) who were linked to the *corteleri* (cutlers), *vagineri* (scabbard-makers), *frezeri* (arrow-makers) and *corazzeri* (armourers). Here the Tana rope factory next to the ship-building Arsenal was granted a monopoly for the manufacture of crossbow strings, in order to ensure consistent quality.

Central Italy had armaments centres too, such as in Tuscany. In fact armourers from northern Italy may have been frequently invited to Florence in the 12th century, including a family which adopted the name of *Acciajoli* or 'men of steel'. This family developed a flourishing armour and banking business, rising to positions of prominence and political power in Tuscany, Naples and Crusader Greece. Florentine armourers formed a subdivision of the Silk Guild which suggests that they were concerned with trading weaponry rather than manufacturing it. Those who actually made armaments were grouped into the minor guilds of *spadari* (sword) and cuirass-makers, *tavolacciai e scudai* (shield-makers), and *fabbri e calderai* (smiths and 'kettle-makers' who also made helmets). Meanwhile

51

cervellari also made all sorts of helmets and *corazzeri* made all sorts of body armour. The statutes or regulations of the Florentine *Arte* (guild) of cuirass-makers, lock-makers, iron-workers and copper-workers were drawn up in 1321 to include all 'those who make cuirasses and all other forms of iron armour': the regulations insisted that anyone who held office in the guilds was a 'good Guelf'. The Statutes of the Florentine *Arte* of leatherworkers was drawn up in 1338 to cover those who manufactured shields, laying great emphasis on the use of good and correct materials. For example, a *pavese, scudo, tabulaccio, rotella, targa, bracciaiuolo* or *broccolerio* could only include horse, ass, cow, bull or pig leather, and not the skins of dogs, wolves or goats. Lines of demarcation were another concern, particularly in dealings with those who made other aspects of arms and armour which included leather elements. Falsification in the making of military items was harshly punished, and only members of the Florentine guild of *corazzeri* and *spadari* were allowed to sign their products with an engraving tool, presumably as a way of ensuring quality control. Lucca in the 14th century employed its own *magistri balistarum* to supervise the construction of crossbows, one such man being a Florentine, Filippo Loni, who was hired on a five-year contract in 1370. Back in 1284 King Charles of Naples ordered large numbers of composite crossbows from Arezzo, while in Lucera the 'Saracen' community included artisans who made similar weapons. Raw materials for the best crossbows came from distant parts, including horn from Alpine regions, wood from the Balkans and cornel or dogwood from the Trabzon area of northern Turkey. Emperor Frederick II of southern Italy and Sicily is said to have imported two-feet crossbows from Palestine in 1239. However, Catalonia and the Balearic islands were a more important source of crossbows, which were generally considered superior to those made in Italy.

Trade in finished arms and armour could involve very large quantities of items and goods. King Charles of Naples for example ordered 4,000 *targe* and *pavesi* shields from Pisa. In 1295 a Lombard merchant brought no fewer than 1,885 crossbows, 666,258 *quarreli*, 6,309 small shields, 2,853 light helmets, 4,511 quilted coats, 751 pairs of gauntlets, 1,374 *gorgiera* neck protectors and brassards, 5,067 coats-of-plates, 13,495 lances or

lanceheads, 1,989 axes and 14,599 swords and *couteaux* daggers to Brugge. According to Neapolitan records from the same period, crossbow *quarreli* were normally transported in wooden crates. Italian crossbows were also sold in the Balkans.

The most famous arms merchant of the 14th century was an Italian named Datini who came from Prato. He described Milan as the 'head of our trade' in armour though most of his swords and daggers came from Florence, Viterbo and Bologna. Datini also traded in sheet-metal for shaping into visors and arm-defences. Many items were purchased in an unfinished state and even Datini's wife was once recorded 'sewing' helmets. He hired equipment to those unable to purchase outright, and sent agents to places where arms and armour were going cheap because fighting had ceased. Successful soldiers would also sell equipment collected on the battlefield and there was a brisk trade in such secondhand arms.

There were large fluctuations in the cost of armaments: considered in isolation the prices mean little, but they can be compared with each other and with other items. For example, in 13th-century Venice a sword was worth 45 crossbow *quarreli*, and a knife worth 25 *quarreli* (one *quarrel* cost around one denarius). In Genoa a mail coif cost between 16 and 32 sous, whereas a mail *hauberk* cost between 120 and 152 sous, presumably reflecting the effort involved in its manufacture. In 1250 the cost was put at 20 soldi for a coif, 120 to 130 for a *hauberk*, but only 45 to 60 soldi for a cuirass which was probably of leather, and 40 to 50 for a *panceria*. By the mid-14th century in Florence 20,000 locally made *viretoni* (crossbow bolts) cost 111 gold florins; while 300 crossbows, 200 *barbuta* helmets, 100 *crocchi* (hooks) to span crossbows and an un-numbered quantity of *viretoni* all came to 700 gold florins. During a similar period Datini sold Milanese *bacinetti* including mail aventails, leather lining and an 'inner hood', for between 4 and 21 florins depending on quality, whereas simple *cervelliere* helmets for infantrymen cost only a mere 33 soldi.

DRESS, WEAPONS AND ARMOUR

France was the centre of fashion for medieval western Europe and Italian dress only really developed its distinctive features during the 14th century. The most common articles of under-garments were made of linen or cotton, consisting of an *interula* or *camicia* for the upper part of the body and a *femorale* for the lower, plus tight-fitting hose. A suit or *indumentum* was worn over these, consisting of the *tunica* or *gonnella* long shirt to the knees, a *pelliccia*, *renonis* or *marzucca* (short coat), or the elegant *guarnacca* and *argoctum*, with or

'Longinus and the Virgin Mary' on a wall-painting in the church of Santa Maria inter Angelus, Spoleto, c. 1300. (Inv. 1924.20, Art Museum, Worcester, Massachusetts; author's photograph)

without sleeves. Finally there were overcoats such as the *mantellum, pelles, par pellium* and *clamys*, often with a *capputium* (hood) attached. These could be buckled on the right shoulder or made of two pieces, and joined on both shoulders. The wealthy indulged themselves with imported silk, lined fabrics and furs, while the poor put up with *pilurica* ('hairy' garments) of rough wool. Increased trade with Russia and the steppes introduced lambskin, though only the poor wore sheepskin, as it was prone to smelling bad. Reduced trade with the Islamic world led to fewer silks while mass-production of fabric in Flanders, Champagne and England reduced the cost of woollen and linen cloth. This is turn led to a fashion for 'covered' furs, with an external layer of decorated fabric.

There was a gradual move away from the flowing robes of earlier years to what has been called 'sculptural simplicity', involving the use of heavier fabrics. The wealthy began to spend so much on ostentatious outdoor costume that governments became worried. In fact a real 'Age of Luxury' dawned in the second quarter of the 14th century. Perhaps the most significant new garment was a short, tight-fitting, padded tunic based upon a form of soft-armour which, according to Italian chroniclers, first appeared in Florence, Rome and Milan in 1302. It was certainly worn in Naples in the 1330s and having been adopted by wealthy young men, spread across the whole of western Europe to be worn by all classes and ages, except the very poorest.

This phenomenon paralleled a militarisation of Western society and was another aspect of the celebration of violence which characterised western Europe for centuries. Male fashions generally became very tight-fitting, emphasising masculinity first by showing the whole leg in skin-tight hose and eventually by padding the genital area. In fact the 14th century saw the total separation of male and female costume, which remains typical of Western society even today. It was also an assertion of male domination and a rejection of any association with neighbouring Byzantine and Islamic civilisations.

Militia regulations did not deal with ordinary dress, but they did of course specify military equipment in detail. In Bologna in 1252 this consisted of an assortment of staff-weapons from spears and javelins to specialised staff-weapons, such as the *penato*, which was like an early *roncone* with a hook on the side, and a long-hafted axe called a *bordone*. Some of these fearsome infantry staff-weapons were weighted with lead to increase their striking power. A Bolognese law of 1288 specified the armour required of militia infantrymen: *panceria* or *caschetto, corsetto* and *manica di ferro* gauntlets, *collare* or *gorgiera, gambiera* and *cervelliera* of mail, *ciroteca* body armour of iron and a good quality *tabulaccio* or *bracciaiuolo* shield. Apart from their crossbows, the weaponry specified for cross-bowmen was much the same.

In the 1280s King Charles of Naples gave orders that each cross-bowman be supplied with a *giubetta* quilted soft armour (possibly with mail inside), a *cervelliera* light helmet, *gorgiera*, *perpunto* (quilted armour), a crossbow with its bandolier and string, a sword, and a *coltello con punta* (pointed dagger). Spearmen were supplied with a *giubetta*, a *gorgiera* 'suitable' for the size of their shield, a spear, *cervelliera*, sword and ordinary form of *coltello*. Archers from the 'Saracens of Lucera' needed more specialised weaponry including bows 'of bone in the manner of the Turks' (composite bows) with *coccari* quivers, the long arrows used with such bows, spears and small, round *rotelle* shields. On some occasions these 'Saracens' were given *spalliere* shoulder protectors, *camici d'armi* (which were probably a sort of uniform coat), and *tacche*, which have provisionally been identified as archer's thumb-rings.

Documents from the 14th century differ only in their reference to newer forms of equipment. By now Italian infantry staff-weapons were highly developed, reflecting their importance in warfare. Whereas the blades of 13th-century infantry spears were from 30 to 45cm long on hafts from two to almost three metres long, some 14th-century versions were considerably longer. The *falce* or *falcione* was a lighter staff-weapon used from the 12th to the 14th century, common amongst urban militias, whereas the complex *ronco* or *roncone* came to prominence as a heavy infantry weapon in the second half of the 13th century. Such weapons were mostly designed to fight cavalry and kill their horses, as were spe-cialised forms of spiked clubs and maces. The broad-bladed *basilarda* thrusting dagger was primarily an infantry weapon, and although there is considerable argument about the origins of its name, the dagger itself was in a tradition of Mediterranean thrusting weapons known in Italy since the 9th century.

Most infantry militiamen could not afford the latest military equipment, and throughout the 13th century mail provided the most common protection for body, neck, arms and legs. The fabric-covered *ghiazzerina*, which also incorporated its own padding, is not recorded in Italy before the early-14th century. On the other hand, early forms of *corellus* or *corettum* cuirass and *lameria* coat-of-plates appeared towards the end of the 13th century. The *paio di corazze*, present in the final third of the 13th century, was a leather cuirass incorporating plates or lames of hardened leather or iron. It was almost certainly of eastern inspiration but was rarely worn by infantry.

Instead many Italian foot soldiers abandoned heavy and inconvenient mail in favour of quilted soft-armour. The infantryman's *strapecta* mentioned in Vercelli in 1220–21 may have been an example, while the *zuppa*, *zupone* or *zuparane*, first mentioned a few years later, was certainly quilted armour though it may also have incorporated mail. The southern Italian *giubetta* was the same garment and a document from Naples, dated 1283, specified that it must be made of fustian cloth or canvas. Like mail, soft-armour offered little protection against arrows but it was light, cheap and

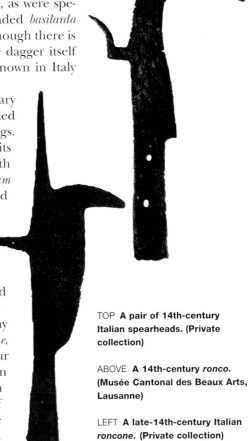

TOP **A pair of 14th-century Italian spearheads. (Private collection)**

ABOVE **A 14th-century *ronco*. (Musée Cantonal des Beaux Arts, Lausanne)**

LEFT **A late-14th-century Italian *roncone*. (Private collection)**

55

**'The Condemnation of St. James'
on a late-13th-century panel of
a silver altar made by Andrea
di Jacopo d'Ognabene. (*In situ*,
Pistoia cathedral; author's
photograph)**

effective against cutting blows. Since a man on horseback could not dodge missile weapons, he was all but obliged to wear the new *piatini* heavy plate-armour once he had abandoned his large shield. The man on foot, however, remained more agile and often still carried one of several versions of large shield. Hence he neither needed, nor wanted the weight of, full plate armour. The lightness of hardened leather armour, and the fact that it was almost as effective as iron, made it similarly popular in 13th- to mid-14th-century Italy. The infantryman was, in fact, often issued with a *coretto* which, in the late-13th century, was probably made of leather and lacked sleeves. In the second half of the 14th century the arms merchant Datini described some *coretti* as having short sleeves and metal studs, suggesting that this term now referred to a *brigandine* which was first mentioned in Italy around 1367 as the '*corazzine brighantine*'.

The first record of leather upper-arm protections was in the *Roman de Meliadus* written by Rusticiano of Pisa around 1265, with pictorial evidence appearing a decade or so later. Separate mail or mail-covered gauntlets appear around the same time, though remaining rarer. By the second half of the 14th century Datini was describing iron gauntlets lined with leather and having tin studs, as well as cuissards and *harnais de jambes* for the legs made of iron or leather with iron studs.

The most important piece of armour was the helmet which was still made of iron rather than steel. Helmets had thicker fronts and tops than sides, though some 14th-century examples also had a thickened area over the vital motor centres of the brain at the back of the head. Several styles were available in Italy, as elsewhere, including the broad-brimmed *cappella di ferro* (or 'iron hat'), in use from the late-12th century. Early in the 13th century the close-fitting *cervelliera* became the most popular form, sometimes worn beneath rather than over a mail *coif*. The *bacinetto* or *bazinetto*, first recorded in Padua in 1281 but present in pictorial sources dating from 20 years earlier, evolved from this and became by far the most common Italian infantry helmet. The *barbuta* was a specialised form of *bacinetto* which came further down the sides of the face. It was first mentioned in the mid-14th century. Concern to protect the face was a major characteristic of Italian armour and might have reflected the importance of the crossbow in Italian warfare. Neck and shoulder armour was obviously important for infantry when facing cavalry, and references to the neck-protecting *gorgiera* become common in the 13th century. A semi-rigid or thickly padded mail or scale shoulder and neck armour used in early-14th-century France and England was called a *pizaine*, which suggests it originally came from Pisa, while in the late-14th century plated versions of the *gorgiera* were developed.

Shields declined in importance for cavalry but remained essential for infantry, evolving into many different forms. Three types were listed for King Charles' expedition against the Aragonese in 1283; *scudi, pavese* and *targhe*. The *targhe* and *pavese* were made of fig or willow wood according to Pisan records, with a leather covering called an *incoriati* or *incollati*. According to one source such shields required two whole ass or horse skins, one for the inside, one for the outside. The *pavese* purchased by Naples in 1282 were 'of five palms' or 'even wider'. The earliest reference to a *pavensibus*, the Latin version of *pavese*, was in Bologna in 1229, but the name came from nearby Pavia, a source of pride to the people of that city. As an anonymous Pavian chronicler wrote around 1330: 'The military renown of the Pavians is proclaimed all over Italy. After it are called the large shields, rectangular at the top and bottom, known as Papienses.'

COLLECTIONS

Surviving military artefacts from 13th–14th-century Italy are scattered amongst several museums, mostly outside Italy itself. Italy is however overflowing with art, much of which dates from the 13th–14th centuries and illustrates soldiers who clearly reflect the militias of the period. The following list only includes relevant Gothic or Early-Renaissance art.

Angera, Rocca Borromeo: late-13th-century
    wall-paintings.
Arezzo, Duomo: 1327–30 carvings on the
    Mausoleum of the Tarlati family.
Assisi, Basilica of San Francesco: late-13th and
    early-14th-century wall-paintings.
Avio, Castello: *c.* 1340 wall-paintings.
Bergamo, Duomo: mid-14th-century carvings and
    wall-paintings.
Bologna, Basilica di Santo Stefano: late-13th-century
    carvings.
Como, Sant'Abbondio: 1330–35 wall-paintings.
Florence, Museo dell'Opera di Santa Croce:
    mid-14th-century wall-paintings. Palazzo Vecchio:
    early-14th-century wall-painting of 'Capture of
    the Duke of Athens'. Santo Spirito: *c.* 1360
    wall-painting by Orcagna.
Fossa, Santa Maria ad Cryptas: 1263, wall-paintings.
Orvieto, Museo dell'Opera del Duomo: 1337
    wall-paintings.

Allegorical figure of 'Law' on an early-14th-century treaty between Prato and the Kingdom of Naples. (Ms. Royal 6.E. IX, f.21, British Library, London)

Padua, Arena Chapel: 1303–6 wall-paintings by Giotto. Oratorio di San Giorgio: 1378–84 wall-paintings by Altichiero and Avanzo. Santo di San Antonio: 1374–9 wall-paintings by Altichiero.

Perugia, 1278 Fontana Maggiore, carvings by Pisano.

Pisa, Camposanto: 14th-century wall-paintings.

Pistoia, Duomo: late-13th and mid-14th-century silver altar.

San Gimignano, Collegiata: mid-14th-century wall-paintings. Museo Civico: wall-paintings c. 1290.

San Sepolcro, Pinacoteca Comunale: 13th-century relief carving.

Siena, Palazzo Pubblico: 14th-century wall-paintings.

Venice, Doge's Palace: 14th-century carved capitals.

Verona, Santa Maria Antica: early-14th-century carvings.

BIBLIOGRAPHY

(Anon. ed.) *Il sabato di San Barnana: La battaglia di Campaldino, 11 giugno 1289* (Milan 1989).

Ancona, C. 'Milizie e condottieri', in G. Einaudi (ed.), *Storia d'Italia, volume quinto. I documenti* (Turin 1973) 642–665.

Backman, C.H. *The Decline and Fall of Medieval Sicily: Politics, religion and economy in the reign of Frederick III, 1296–1337* (Cambridge 1995).

Benini, S. 'The bow in Italy', *Journal of the Society of Archer-Antiquaries* XXXVI (1993) 7–13.

Blair, C. and Boccia, L.G. *Armi e Armature* (Milan 1981).

Boccia, L.G. and Coelho, E.T. 'L'armamento di cuoio e ferro nel trecento Italiano', *L'Illustrazione italiana* I/2 (1972) 24–27.

Boccia, L.G. and Scalini, M. (eds.) *Guerre e assoldati in Toscana, 1260–1364* (Florence 1982).

Boccia, L.G. *I Guerrieri di Avio* (Milan 1991).

Bowsky, W.M. 'City and Contado: Military Relationships and Communal Bonds in Fourteenth Century Siena', in A. Molho and J.A. Tedeschi (eds.), *Renaissance Studies in Honor of Hans Baron* (Dekalb 1971) 75–98.

Bowsky, W.M. *A Medieval Italian Commune: Siena under the Nine, 1287–1355* (Los Angeles 1981).

Calvini, N. *Balestre e balestieri medievali in Liguria* (San Remo 1982).

Canestrini, G. 'Della milizia italiana dal secolo XIII al XVI', *Archivio Storico Italiano* XV (1851).

Cardini, F. and Salvini, E. *Montaperti 1260, Guerra, Società ed Errori* (Siena 1984).

Cardini, F. and Tangheroni, M. (eds.) *Guerra e Guerrieri nella Toscana Medievale* (Florence 1990).

Cherubini, G. *Signori, Contadini, Borghesi: Ricerche sulla società Italiana del Basso Medioevo* (Florence 1974).

Ciampoli, D. *Il Capitano del Popolo a Siena nel primo Trecento* (Siena 1984).

Colombo, A. *Milano feudale e comunale* (Milan 1928).

Cox, E.L. *The Green Count of Savoy, Amadeus VI and Transalpine Savoy in the Fourteenth Century* (Princeton 1967).

Dini, V. *Dell'Antico Uso della Balestra in Gubbio, San Sepolcro, Massa Marittima e nella Repubblica di San Marino* (Arezzo 1961).

Dondi, G. 'Del Roncone, del Pennato e del cosidetto Scorpione: loro origini', *Armi Antiche* (Turin 1976) 11–48.

Epstein, S.A. *Genoa and the Genoese 959–1528* (Chapel Hill 1996).

Galletti, A.I. 'La società comunale di fronte alla guerra nelle fonti perugine del 1282', *Bollettino della Deputazione di Storia Patria per l'Umbria* LXXI (1974) 35–98.

Hall, A.R. 'Guido's Texaurus, 1335', in B.S. Hill and D.C. West (eds.) *On Pre-Modern Technology and Science. A Volume of Studies in Honor of Lynn White Jr.* (Malibu 1976) 11–35.

Herlihy, D. *Pisa in the Early Renaissance: A Study of Urban Growth* (New Haven 1958).

Herlihy, D., Lopez, R.S. and Slessarev, V. (eds.) *Economy, Society and Government in Medieval Italy: Essays in Memory of Robert L. Reynolds* (Kent, Ohio 1969).

Housley, N. 'The Mercenary Company, the Papacy and the Crusades 1356–1378', *Traditio* XXXVIII (1982) 253–280.

Housley, N. *The Italian Crusades* (Oxford 1982).

Hyde, J.K. *Padua in the Age of Dante* (Manchester 1966).

Hyde, J.K. *Society and Politics in Medieval Italy: The Evolution of Civil Strife, 1000–1350* (London 1973).

Larner, J. *Italy in the Age of Dante and Petrarch 1216–1380* (London 1992).

Martines, L. (ed.) *Violence and Civil Disorder in Italian Cities 1200–1500* (Los Angeles 1972).

Meek, C. *Lucca 1369–1400: Politics and Society in an Early Renaissance City-State* (Oxford 1978).

Minieri-Riccio, C. 'Memorie della guerra di Sicilia negli anni 1282, 1283, 1284, Tratte dai registri Angioini dell'archivio di Stato di Napoli', *Archivio Storico per la Provincia Napolitana* (1876) 85–105, 275–315, 499–530.

Oerter, H.L. 'Campaldino, 1289', *Speculum* XXXIII (1968) 429–450.

Origo, I. *The Merchant of Prato* (reprint London 1963).

Paoli, C. *La Battaglia di Montaperti* (Siena 1869).

Petrovic, D. 'Un Balestiere marchigiano a Ragusa nel XIV secolo', *Quaderni Storici* XIII (1970) 233–245.

Pieri, P. 'Alcune quistioni sopra la fanteria in Italia nel periodo comunale', *Rivista Storica Italiana* L (1933) 561–614.

Pieri, P. 'L'Evoluzione delle Milizie Comunali Italiane', in Pieri, P. *Scritti Vari* (Turin 1966) 31–91.

Romiti, A. 'Le gare di tiro: la balestra, lo schioppetto e lo archibugio', in (anon. ed.) *Alcuni giuochi a Lucca al tempo della repubblica* (Lucca 1981).

Salvemini, S. *I balestieri nel Comune di Firenze* (Bari 1905, reprint Bologna 1967).

Seitz, H. 'La Storta – the Falchion', *Armi Antiche* (Turin 1963).

Settia, A.A. *Comuni in guerra. Armi ed eserciti nell'Italia della città* (Bologna 1993).

Tangheroni, M. *1284, L'anno della Meloria* (Pisa 1984).

Troso, M. *Le Armi in Asta delle Fanterie Europee (1000–1500)* (Novara 1988).

Varanini, G.M. (ed.) *Gli Scaligeri 1277–1387* (Verona 1988).

Waley, D.P. 'Condotte and Condottieri in the Thirteenth Century', *Proceedings of the British Academy* LXI (1975) 337–371.

Waley, D.P. 'The Army of the Florentine Republic from the Twelfth to the Fourteenth Century', in Rubinstein, N. (ed.) *Florentine Studies: Politics and Society in Renaissance Florence* (London 1968) 70–108.

Waley, D.P. *The Papal State in the Thirteenth Century* (London 1961).

Zug Tucci, H. 'Il carroccio nelle vita comunale italiana', *Quellen und Forschungen aus italienische Archiven und Bibliotheken* LXV (1985).

Genoa in the late 13th century with family alliances grouped according to Ghibelline, Guelf or unspecified allegiance. 1 – Calvi and Pallavicini; 2 – Advocate and Pevere; 3 – Grimaldi and Spinola; 4 – De Nigro and De Mari; 5 – Spinola di Luccoli; 6 – De Mari; 7 – Imperiali; 8 – Doria; 9 – Fieschi; 10 – De Volta; 11 – Stregiaporci; 12 – De Castro Embriaci.

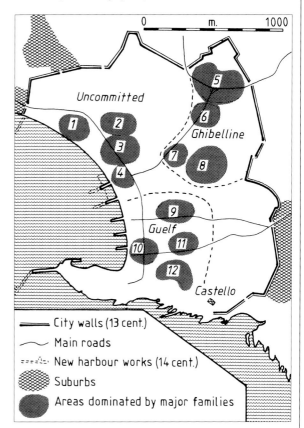

GLOSSARY

The following selection of technical, predominantly early Italian terms provides a basic scheme of reference and explanation for the key words that appear in the text, and that may be encountered in further reading on this subject. Inevitably, the differences and inconsistency between the spellings and the forms of many of the words is a reflection of the evolutionary state of the Italian language at this time. During the 12th, 13th and 14th centuries, almost every region within the physical confines of the Italian peninsular witnessed a further independent divergence in the degeneration of spoken Latin into a particular regional dialect. They did however retain a certain common familiarity and a fair degree of overall inter-comprehension between them, having originated from the same root. It was not until the 15th century that a concerted attempt was made to recognise a standard form of Italian that could be used and understood on a wider scale, initially on a purely diplomatic level. Thus the following list lays no claims to being an absolute, exact guide on the terminology of this subject, but is instead merely intended to aid the reader in what can be a difficult area of research.

Alabarda halbard staff-weapon

Almugavar Catalan and Aragonese light infantry of Moorish origin

Arceri archers.

Arengo a town assembly

Argoctum coat, sometimes of fur

Arte a trade guild

Ascia de fante poleaxe

Bacinetto, bazineto form of helmet protecting the back of the neck

Balcanelle practice target crossbow bolt

Balestieri della Ghiera crossbowmen recruited in the Florentine *contado*

Balestra a crocco crossbow spanned by a hook on a waist belt

Balestra a leva crossbow spanned by a *gaffle* lever

Balestra a staffa stirrup-type crossbow

Balestra da due piedi 'two-feet' crossbow, where both feet are used to hold it while spanning it

Balestra de corno crossbow with a composite bow

Balestra de fusto simple wooden crossbow

Balestra de streva crossbow with an iron stirrup

Balestra de torno crossbow spanned by a *cranequin* or winch, sometimes mounted on a frame

Balestieri crossbowmen

Balestra de pessarolo probably a large crossbow spanned by a winch

Banderia a military unit

Bandifer commander of a Florentine crossbow unit

Barbuta form of helmet protecting the sides of the face

Barsaglandum shooting range

Basilarda dagger with a broad, triangular blade

Bastita fortified village or stockade

Bastone di ferro an iron mace

Bastone di legno a wooden club

Battifolle a wooden siege tower

Berdica a long-hafted axe

Birri élite militia force which also acted as 'police' in Siena

Bordone a long-hafted axe

Bracciaiuolo shield with arm straps

Brigandi Italian infantry, probably of rural or 'brigand' origin

Brigandine a tunic of padded body protection

Broccolerio a shield

Calotta leather lining of a helmet

Camaglio mail aventail

Camicia shirt or undershirt

Campo de batalia militia training ground

Capironi mail *coif*

Capitano del Popolo paid official in command of urban militias

Capituli treaties of submission by feudal lords to the city of Siena

Capo a helmet, or hat

Cappella di ferro an iron-brimmed 'war hat'

Capputium a hood

Carroccio a special cart with a flag and bell, used as a symbol of communal identity

Casa-fondaco house incorporating shops or workshops

Casa-torre house with a fortified tower

Casco; caschetto helmet

Castellan official in charge of a fortified village or castle

Castello fortified village or castle

Cavallata a raid

Cerne Luccan rural militia

Cervellario a helmet-maker

Cervelliera a close-fitting helmet

Ciroteca torso protection

Cistarelle probably leg protectors made of wood, for militia exercises

Cittadini citizens of a city or town

Clamys overcoat

Coccari a form of quiver for arrows

Coif a close-fitting cap of cloth or mail

Collare neck protection

Coltello dagger

Coltello con punta pointed dagger

Comitivo private armed following of a powerful individual in Sicily

Comune system of government in which authority was shared on a quasi-democratic basis

Comunanzo non-aristocratic members of a *comune*

Condotta contract between mercenary troops and employers

Coniuratio sworn association to work for the common good

Consortia a network of families related on both the male and female side

Constable official in charge of maintaining law and order

Consulo political representative

Contadini peasant inhabitants of a *contado*

Contado region around a city ruled by that city

Contrada small ward or precinct in Siena

Corazza; corrazina early form of semi-rigid body armour

Corazzeri armourers

Corazzine brighantine semi-rigid armour of small scales inside fabric covering

Corellus; corettum cuirass or coat-of-plates

Coretto body armour, probably of leather

Cornamusa a wind instrument used in militia bands

Corsesca infantry staff-weapon

Corsetto body armour

Corteleri knife-makers

Coxaroni cuisses, or thigh armour

Cranequin rack and pinion device for spanning a crossbow

Crocco a hook, used to span a bow

Cuir-bouilli hardened leather used to make armour

Decene garrison duty outside a city

Domus [magna] large house of an aristocratic or wealthy family

Electos specially selected élite of militia crossbowmen

Espringal see *spingarda*

Exercitus extended campaign, literally meaning 'army'

Fabbro a smith

Falce da guerra a staff-weapon

Falcione staff-weapon

Falsador a simple crossbow bolt

Femorale undergarment for lower part of body

Ferrari iron-workers

Frezero an arrow-maker

Gaffle metal lever used to span lighter crossbows

Gambiera mail leg protectors

Gastaldiones leaders of Paduan guild militias

Ghiazzerina fabric-covered mail body armour (from the Arabic *khazagand*)

Ghibelline supporter of the Emperor in quarrels with Papacy

Giubbetta quilted soft armour (from the Arabic *jubbah*)

Giupon padded jacket of the 14th century (from the Arabic *jubbah*)

Gonfaloni militia companies

Gonfaloniere officer in command of a militia unit

Gonnella a long shirt

Gorgiera neck-protecting armour

Guaite militia obligation to defend city walls

Gualdane raiding tactics

Guarnacca a coat

Guastatori the infantry used to ravage enemy territory (literally 'spoilers')

Guelf supporter of the Papacy in quarrels with the Emperor

Hauberk a coat of mail

Indumentum a 'suit' of three garments

Interula an undergarment for the upper part of the body

Iuvenes inferioris artisan and worker sections of urban society

Lameria coat-of-plates body armour

Lanzelonghe long infantry spears

Lorica mail *hauberk*

Magistri balistarum a 'master crossbowman' who supervised the construction, maintenance and repair of crossbows

Manaria war-axe

Maniberge mail sleeves covering the hands

Manica di ferro iron gauntlets

Mantellum overcoat

Marinella bell on a *carroccio*

Marzucca short coat of Sardinian origin

Maschera face protection, usually of mail

Masnada following of a military leader

Miles; milites knights, later including the wealthier urban middle class

Monstrà registration where soldiers present themselves, their followers and their horses at a military encampment

Noveschi Siena's guild-based governing body, composed of nine (*nove*) members

Nut a revolving piece set into the stock of a crossbow which releases the bowstring

Osbergum mail *hauberk*

Padiglione mail aventail

Paio di corazze leather cuirass or coat-of-plates

Panceria smaller form of mail armour

Pantera light wagon used to construct field fortifications

Par pellium an overcoat

Partigiana staff-weapon

Paterfamilia technical head of a family, recognised by law

Pavesari infantrymen with a large mantlet-shield

Pavese tall mantlet-shield which was rested on the ground

Pedites infantry

Pelles overcoat

Pelliccia short coat

Penato specialised staff-weapon with a hook on one side, similar to the *ronco*

Pennonieri junior officers

Perpunto quilted soft armour

Piatini plate armour

Pieve group of parishes in the Florentine *contado*

Pilurica rough, coarse-wool garments worn by the poor

Pinions flights of a crossbow bolt (arrow)

Podestà paid official recruited to 'rule' an urban or rural community

Podestarile an urban police district under the control of the *Podestà*

Popolo rule by the non-aristocratic, urban middle class (the *popolani*)

Popolo Grasso members of greater guilds

Popolo Minuto members of minor guilds

Posse militia formation charged with maintaining law and order

Priori guild-based governing body in Florence, composed of the wealthier citizens

Provost official in charge of maintaining law and order

Pugna infantry militia training exercise

Quarrel crossbow bolt (arrow) with a four-sided head

Renonis a short coat

Ribaldi those who manned siege engines (literally 'ruffians')

Ricordi books of family advice and particulars, passed on between generations

Rocca a castle in a raised location

Ronco, roncone bill or staff-weapon

Ronzini pack horses

Rotella small round shield

Rumor military alarm or summons

Salme measure of volume (equivalent to eight barrels)

Scagni a pedestal to support larger types of crossbow

Scudai shield-makers

Scuderi shield carrier

Scudo general term for a shield

Servitia debita military obligation owed by citizens to the state

Sesto Florentine city quarter

Signoria aristocratic rule under one man (a *signore*)

Societas militum the 'society of knights', a political faction

Societas peditum the 'society of foot soldiers', a political faction

Societas populi the 'society of the people', a political faction

Societates armorum armed militia companies

Soldieri poor men who took the place of wealthier militiamen for payment

Spadaccino a light-infantry foot soldier

Spadaro sword-maker

Spalliere shoulder protectors

Spiedo javelin or infantry spear

Spingarda large crossbow-type siege weapon

Spontone, spuntone short infantry spear

Springald see *spingarda*

Stipendia militum obligation for militia service

Stipendiari 'foreign' professional troops on a city's payroll

Strapecta quilted soft-armour worn on the torso

Tabulacciari shield carriers

Tabulaccio large shield

Tacca an archer's thumb ring

Tallia militum tax paid instead of militia service

Targa a small shield

Tavolacciai shield-makers

Terra de arcubus crossbow range

Torre urban or rural fortified tower

Trombetta military trumpet

Tubatores official trumpeters of a *comune*

Tunica long shirt, almost to the knees, for men

Vagineri scabbard and sheath-makers

Valvassori knights

Vastatori see *guastatori*

Vendetta officially recognised system of controlled vengeance

Venticinquina militia unit of twenty-five men

Verga sardesca infantry javelin of Sardinian origin

Vessilli militia unit with nominal allegiance to a particular banner (*vexillum*)

Vexillum military unit banner

Viretoni crossbow bolt designed to spin in the air

Xurteri night-watch militia companies in Palermo

Zuppa; zupone, zuparane quilted armour (from the Arabic *jubbah*)

61

THE PLATES

PLATE A: GENOESE *PAVESARI* TRAINING, c. 1260

Apart from target practice by crossbowmen, foot soldiers including *pavesari* took part in *pugne*, or 'fights'. Teams from various quarters of the city probably formed shield walls which pressed against each other in something like a rugby scrum. Wooden clubs were used instead of real weapons while a judge tried to ensure that the exercise did not degenerate into a brawl.

PLATE B: MILITIA CROSSBOWMAN AND HIS WEAPONRY, c. 1275

B1: The main figure wears a one-piece iron *cervelliera*, a mail-lined linen *coif* and a padded mail *gorgiera* around his neck and shoulders. Beneath his sleeveless mail *panceria* he has a thickly padded *perpunto*. In addition to quilted cuisses over his thighs he has greaves made of plaited willow, probably called *cistarelle*.

B2: Section through a simple *cervelliera* showing the leather lining.

B3: Mail-lined and padded linen *coif*.

B4: *Gorgiera* viewed from rear, showing lacing and lining.

B5: Presumed structure of a simple *ciroteca* of rawhide.

B6: Quilted cuisses over breeches, held by a drawstring through the waistband.

B7: Possible construction of a *cistarella* greave made of plaited willow.

B8: *Coltello* or early *basilarda* in which the blade and hilt form an integral whole covered with shaped pieces of wood; plus details of the inner and outer faces of the sheath.

B9: Disassembled elements of a sword with the inner and outer faces of its scabbard showing attachment of the sword-belt.

A: mail lining of a padded *coif* from Provence, 1250–1300. (Inv. H5, Musée de l'Armée, Paris)

B: late-14th/early-15th-century Italian *bacinetto*, cut down at a later date. (State Historical Museum, Conservation Store, Moscow; author's photograph)

C: mid-14th-century Italian *bacinetto*, later cut down with 'eye slots'. (Inv. 29.158, 44, Metropolitan Museum of Art, New York)

D: mid-14th-century northern Italian *bacinetto*, with the rear cut away. (Private collection)

B10: Interior of the shield with leather covering a wooden base.

B11: Exterior of the shield, painted with the arms of the Borgo quarter of Florence.

B12: Crossbow and bolt.

PLATE C: THE BATTLE OF CAMPALDINO, 1289

In the Florentine victory over their rival Arezzo at Campaldino, infantry formed the flanks of the Florentine battle-line. The Arezzo cavalry charged across their front, aiming for the Florentine cavalry at the centre, which also had light infantry among them. Here Florentine crossbowmen and *pavesari* are skirmishing ahead of their simple field-fortifications.

PLATE D: CROSSBOWS AND ASSOCIATED EQUIPMENT

D1: Primitive Alpine crossbow, 11th–12th centuries, with simple wooden bow and a vertical peg to release the string.

D2: Standard composite crossbow of the 13th–14th centuries with a parchment-covered composite bow, a revolving nut carved from horn and an iron stirrup.

D3: Large 'two feet' crossbow with a vertical peg and wooden trigger.

D4: Steel crossbow with a much shorter span and thus shorter stock or tiller.

D5: Details of the construction of a crossbow [A–B middle, C–G top left, H–I bottom of page]. A: unknotted string. B: knotted string. C: side and front views of nut showing groove for the bolt and the notch for trigger. D: section through one type of composite crossbow (1, parchment; 2, sinew lengthways along the bow; 3, wooden core; 4, vertical strips of horn lengthways along the bow; 5, sinew around the bow). E: sectional view of the attachment of a steel bow to its stock (i, bow; (ii), packing piece to stop chaffing. F: top view of packing piece. G: end of stock with bow removed. H: iron stirrup. I: later form of stirrup.

D6: Trigger mechanisms. (a), peg with trigger raised. (b), peg with trigger lowered. (c), nut and sprung trigger system in shooting position. (d), nut and sprung trigger in loose position.

D7: (i): early form of crossbow arrow (smaller scale than bolts). (ii): bolts with feather flights. (iii): bolt with leather flights.

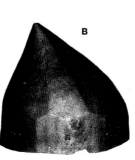

A

B

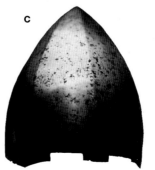

C

D

PLATE E: CROSSBOW SPANNING SYSTEMS

E1: Spanning large 'two feet' crossbow using hands.
E2: Spanning composite crossbow with stirrup and belt hook.
E3: Using a single cord pulley.
E4: Using a *gaffle* or 'Goat's Foot' lever.
E5: Spanning a steel crossbow using a *cranequin*.
E6: Using a windlass.
E7: Single spanning hook attached to a leather belt.
E8–10: Alternative methods of attaching hook to belt.
E11: Double spanning hook.
E12: Single cord, single pulley, single hook system.
E13: Doubled pulley device.
E14: Linked iron pulleys for double cord device.
E15: Single pulley system attached to crossbow.
E16: Bronze 'roller pulley'.
E17: *Gaffle* attached to crossbow.
E18: Iron *gaffle*.
E19: Iron windlass.
E20: Bronze *cranequin* with a thick rope loop attached to box.

PLATE F: MILITIAMAN OF LUCCA SUMMONED FROM HIS SHOP, c. 1310

Most urban infantry militiamen were drawn from the ranks of skilled artisans and shopkeepers. Such men could be summoned at very short notice though a full-scale military expedition would entail more warning. They would then be selected by ballot or in rotation, since the system was designed not to disrupt the commercial life of the city.

PLATE G: PROFESSIONAL PAVESARE AND HIS WEAPONRY, c. 1335

G1: Many of medieval Italy's best infantry came from mountainous regions. This figure is largely based upon the wall-paintings in the Casa dei Soldati in Avio castle between Verona and Trento.
G2: Alternative blades for staff-weapons.
G3: Alternative heads for *lanzelonge*.
G4: Section through *bacinetto* showing the leather lining or *calotta*.
G5: *Bacinetto* with hat worn over the top.

G6: Long and short forms of quilted soft armour.
G7: Coat-of-plates with part of fabric removed.
G8: Padded leather gauntlet partially covered in mail with a drawstring to tighten the wrist.
G9: Interior of *pavese* with upper strap for the elbow, middle strap for the wrist, and lower strap for the fist.
G10: *Pavese* with the arms of the Castelbarco family.
G11: *Basilarda* with its sheath.
G12: Purse.

PLATE H: *CARROCCIO* AND TRANSPORT EQUIPMENT

H1: Sienese *carroccio* with a *marinella* bell. A: view of the right-hand horse attached to the *carroccio*; note that it has a saddle for a man to ride 'post' so that the wagon needs no driver. B: the left-hand horse, showing the pole to which both horses are harnessed, and that runs between them.
H2: Flat-topped wagon pulled by oxen.
H3: Mule with the simplest form of pack-saddle and sacks, one with a merchant's stencilled ownership mark.
H4: Baggage donkey with a wooden yoke beneath its tail to stop the pack-saddle slipping forwards when going downhill.
H5: Open wagon pulled by a pair of oxen and one horse.
H6: Wooden yoke for a pair of oxen.

PLATE I: URBAN WARFARE IN THE ADIGE VALLEY, c.1345

The militiamen defending this barricade are based upon Guelf soldiers in the wall-paintings at Avio castle: the knight leading their foes is from the Ghibelline faction. The *spingarda* pictured in the bottom right of the plate was powered by twisted skeins of horsehair.

PLATE J: LIGHT INFANTRY *SPADACCINO* IN PAPAL SERVICE, c. 1375

J1: This foot soldier has the most up-to-date arms and armour available, though as a light infantryman he has no leg armour and relies upon his large oval shield.
J2: Rear of helmet and *brigandine* showing buckled strap from helmet.
J3: Interior of the *brigandine*, plus to the right a section

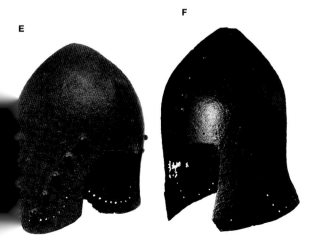

E

F

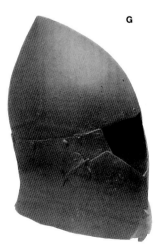

G

E: mid-14th-century Italian *bacinetto* from Naples. (British Museum, London)
F: 14th-century Italian *bacinetto*. (Askeri Muzesi, Istanbul; author's photograph)
G: late-14th/early-15th-century Italian helmet from Khalkis. (Historical Museum, Athens; author's photograph)

through the *brigandine* showing layers of cloth, and part of the exterior with fabric removed.

J4: Defences for left arm. 1, gauntlet of moulded *cuir-bouilli*. 2, single sheet of *cuir-bouilli* for upper arm. 3, multiple armour for elbow and lower arm of *cuir-bouilli* and leather covered strips of iron. 4, interior of the lower arm piece.

J5: Interior of the shield showing leather-covered laminated wooden structure.

J6: Exterior of shield.

J7: Dagger and sheath.

J8: *Stocco* sword.

PLATE K: GENOESE MERCHANT SHIP ATTACKED BY PIRATES, c. 1390

The tall wooden 'castles' at the stern and prow of such ships held the key to their defence, where *pavesari* could protect the captain from sharpshooters. Nevertheless some of the larger weapons used in naval warfare, such as 'great crossbows', could penetrate bulwarks, shields and, it was said, several men.

PLATE L: NON-MILITARY CLOTHING

L1: Late-13th-century underclothes.

L2: Late-14th-century underclothes.

L3: Shirts and tunics. 1, white linen shirt with a wooden button. 2, Italian shirt of the 14th century. 3, fur-lined tunic; note the pockets are merely holes. 4, long tunic of the 14th century, partially lined with fur. 5, long tunic with a tall quilted collar.

L4: Long and short versions of the quilted *perpunto*.

L5: Hoods and hats. (i) woollen hood with short tail thrown fowards. (ii) fur-lined hat with outer fabric in heraldic colours. (iii) front and side views of a conical hat with top tucked into the brim before drooping down the side. (iv) simple woollen cap. (v) cap with decorated brim. (vi) felt hat with brim pushed forward. (vii) exceptionally tall hat with brim turned up and down while the cone is folded side to side.

L6: Shoes and boots. 1, open leather sandal with fabric around the heel. 2, buckled leather sandal. 3, soft leather boot. 4, leather shoe covered with cloth. 5, plain leather shoe. 6, long-toed shoe.

Carving of a foot soldier by Giovanni de Campione, dating from 1360. (*In situ*, south portal of Santa Maria Maggiore, Bergamo; author's photograph)